INTRODUCING THE ELEMENTARY ENGLISH LANGUAGE ARTS
(Second Edition)

JAMES KILLORAN

STUART ZIMMER

MARK JARRETT

JARRETT PUBLISHING COMPANY

EAST COAST OFFICE
P.O. Box 1460
19 Cross Street
Ronkonkoma, NY 11779
631-981-4248

WEST COAST OFFICE
10 Folin Lane
Lafayette, CA 94549
925-906-9742

1-800-859-7679   Fax: 631-588-4722
www.jarrettpub.com

Grateful acknowledgment is made to the following to reprint the copyrighted materials listed below:

Alfred A. Knopf, Inc. for "City" by Langston Hughes in *The Collected Poems of Langston Hughes,* © 1994. August House for the story, "Old Joe and the Carpenter" in *Thirty Three Multi-cultural Tales To Tell,* edited by Pleasant DeSpain. Children's Better Health Institute for the article in *Child Life,* "Happy Birthday, Basketball" by Charles Davis in the March, 2000 issue. Cobblestone Publishing Company for the article in *Appleseeds Magazine,* "Pass the Bread, Please" by Cyndy Hall in the February, 1999 issue. Harcourt, Brace, and Company for *Half Magic,* by Edward Eager, © 1954. *Highlights For Children* for: the story "The Recital" by Kathleen Benner Duble, in the February, 1999 issue; the story "Carrie Rose Hated Red" by Susan Uhlig, in the April, 2000 issue; the story "Come Rain or Shine" a folktale retold by Geary Smith, in the March, 1995 issue; the article, "Chopsticks" by Samantha Bonar, in the September, 1995 issue; the article "Calm Under Fire: The Story of Henry Flipper" by Bea Bragg in the February, 1999 issue; the article "Treasure Hunter" by Ellen Hobart in the May, 2000 issue; the article "The Wandering Continent" by Eon Bilokur, in the June, 1955 issue; the article "The Cold Facts about Ice Cream" by Kristin Martelle in the August, 1996 issue. Scholastic, Inc. for the article in *Scholastic Update,* "The Celebrated Deformed Frogs" by Susan Hayes, in the April 13, 1998 issue. Simon and Schuster for the story, "Tashira's Turn" in *The Children's Book of Heroes* edited by William Bennett © 1997. John Wiley and Sons, for *Science Around the Year* by Janice Cleave © 2000.

Copyright 2001 by Jarrett Publishing Company

ISBN 1-882422-60-0
Printed in the United States of America
by Malloy Lithographing, Inc., Ann Arbor, Michigan
First Edition
10 9 8 7 6 5 4 3 2   04 03 02 01

ACKNOWLEDGMENTS

The authors would like to thank the following educators who helped review the manuscript. Their collective comments, suggestions, and recommendations have proved invaluable in preparing this book.

Elaine Mallor
Reading Teacher at Merrimac Elementary School
Holbrook, New York

Ruth Townsend
Teacher at Manhattanville College
Purchase, New York
English Language Arts Consultant, N.Y.S.E.C. Teacher of Excellence
Director for the National Council of Teachers of English (Region 1)

Tina Zeltmann
Third Grade Teacher at Remsenburg-Speonk Elementary School
Remsenburg, New York

Cover design, layout, graphics, and typesetting:
Burmar Technical Corporation, Albertson, N.Y.

This book is dedicated…

to my wife Donna and my children Christian, Carrie, and Jesse

— *James Killoran*

to my wife Joan, my children Todd and Ronald, and
my grandchildren Jared and Katie

— *Stuart Zimmer*

to my wife Gośka and my children Alexander and Julia

— *Mark Jarrett*

Other books by Killoran, Zimmer, and Jarrett
Mastering New York's Grade 4 English Language Arts Test
Mastering New York's Grade 8 English Language Arts Test
Mastering the Grade 3 ISAT Reading and Writing Tests
Mastering the Grade 5 ISAT Reading and Writing Tests
Mastering Ohio's Fourth Grade Proficiency Tests in Reading and Writing
Mastering the Grade 3 MCAS Reading Test
Mastering the Grade 4 MCAS Tests in English Language Arts
Mastering the Grade 4 FCAT Reading and Writing Test
Mastering the Elementary English Language Arts

TABLE OF CONTENTS

UNIT 1: READING

UNIT 1: READING

In this unit, you will learn some new ways to become a better reader and to perform better on reading tests. You will also learn to recognize different types of readings and what to look for in each type. The most important thing is to be an active reader. By connecting what you read to what you already know, you will better understand what you read.

CHAPTER 1

HOW TO BE
A GOOD READER

Are you a good reader? You probably first began to read by sounding out or memorizing words. However, recognizing words is just the beginning of being a good reader. The most important part of reading is **understanding** the ideas of the writer and seeing how these fit in with your own ideas.

You should try to become an **active** reader. You interact with what you read by asking questions. Think about how the author's ideas match up with your own ideas. This interacting with what you read helps you to understand the reading better. In this chapter, you will learn some important ways of better understanding what you read.

READING STRATEGIES

A **strategy** is a plan for winning a game or achieving a goal. Just as a coach uses a strategy to win a game, good readers use special strategies when they read. Experts in reading have identified several **reading strategies.** These strategies are used by good readers to better understand and apply what they read.

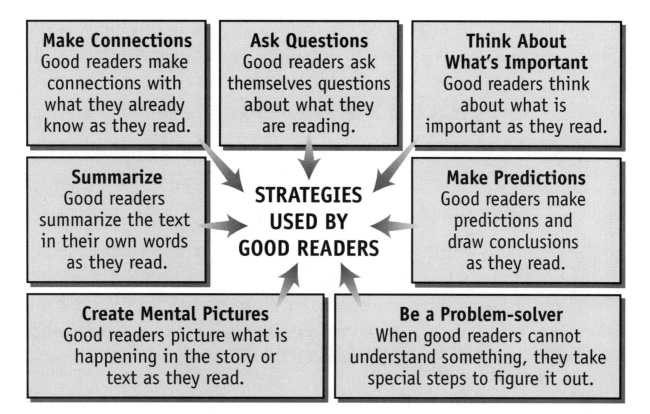

These seven strategies are used throughout the reading process. They include things you should do *before, during,* and *after* you read any reading selection. This chapter will look more closely at how these strategies work.

BEFORE READING

When you are about to read something, you should always ask yourself:

★ *Why am I reading this selection?*

★ *What do I already know about this subject?*

Think about *why* you are reading the story or reading passage. For example, is it to find out specific information or to enjoy a good story? Next, look over the title and the text to get some general idea of what the reading is about. See if there are illustrations, headings, or other clues about the subject of the reading. Then think about what you already know about that type of reading and its subject matter.

Finally, think of any questions you may have about the reading or its subject matter. What would you like to find out about that topic?

DURING READING

As you read, *make connections, ask questions,* and *make predictions.* You should also think about what is important and create mental images — pictures in your mind — as you read.

 Make Connections. Ask yourself if what you are reading reminds you of something you already know. This could be something you experienced in your life or something you read or heard about. See how well the reading compares to what you already know or have experienced.

 Ask Questions. Good readers ask themselves questions about what they are reading. For example, good readers ask **what** is happening in the reading. They ask **why** things in the story happen the way they do. Asking questions helps you focus on what you are reading. You will learn more about asking questions in the next chapter.

Think about What Is Important. What is important in a reading will depend both on the reading itself and on your purpose for reading it. As you read, focus on the author's main ideas or key events in the story. As you read each detail, ask yourself if it is important to the overall meaning of the story or passage.

Often, important parts of the text will be identified for you. The title is important because it tells you what the passage is about. Headings, **bold** print, words in *italics* or in CAPITAL letters are usually important. Many paragraphs will have **topic sentences** stating the main idea of the paragraph.

Create Mental Pictures. Much of what we know about the world comes from our five senses. Therefore, when you read, try to picture the things you are reading about. For example, imagine you are listening as each story character speaks. Picture what it would be like to smell, taste, or touch what a character is experiencing.

Make Predictions. Good readers make predictions about what will come next. For example, if you are reading a story and the main character faces a problem, you might think about some of the ways the problem could be solved.

Summarize. Good readers often pause to think about what they have just read. They silently summarize what is important in their own words. They check details to make sure their summary is correct before they read on.

Be a Problem-Solver. When good readers have trouble understanding something, they take steps to figure it out. They may re-read a difficult section one or more times to make sure they understand it.

AFTER READING

After you finish a reading, think about what you have just read. Think back about what was **most important** in the reading. Mentally **summarize** what the reading was about. Think about what you learned from the reading, and how it fits in with what you know.

To become a good reader, you should ask yourself the following:

★ What was the message or main idea of the reading?

★ Have I learned something *new*?

★ What were some "memorable" words or phrases?

SAMPLE MODEL

Let's see how a good reader uses these strategies with an actual reading. Read the passage below about the history of ice cream.

BEFORE READING

Before reading this passage, ask yourself:

> *Why am I reading this selection?* I am reading this passage to find out how people first started eating ice cream, one of my favorite foods.
>
> *What do I already know about this subject?* Today we make ice cream with freezers. I don't know how they made ice cream in earlier times.

DURING READING

Here are some of the things a good reader might be thinking about while reading this article on the history of ice cream.

MAKE CONNECTIONS
I already know what ice cream is. The title tells me I will learn some other "cool facts" about ice cream.

MAKE PREDICTIONS
From the text, I can tell this is an article, not a story. I predict the article will tell me more about the history of ice cream.

The Daily Journal

THE COLD FACTS ABOUT ICE CREAM
by Kristin Martelle

The first evidence of any kind of frozen sweets is from Alexander the Great in the fourth century B.C. Legend has it that this mighty leader enjoyed icy drinks. Once, he even had thirty trenches filled with snow to chill drinks for ladies' refreshment.

CREATE MENTAL IMAGES
I can just imagine Alexander's troops filling the trenches with snow in order to chill the drinks.

ASK QUESTIONS
As I read, I ask the following questions:

❏ What does *savor* mean?

❏ What else did Roman emperors want served at royal feasts?

❏ How did the Romans keep the snow from melting?

❏ Did Nero really execute the general?

Roman emperors savored fruit pulps and juices flavored with honey and chilled with ice and snow. Emperor Nero demanded these "ices" be served at royal feasts. But getting snow from the faraway Alps was a challenge. Ways to keep the ice from melting were planned months in advance. Runners raced hundreds of miles to get their ice to Rome. Legend has it that once, when the snow melted before it reached Nero he executed the general in command.

By the year 1500, cream had been added to the recipes, and Italian nobles couldn't get enough "cream ice." The "cream ice" was brought to France in 1533 with the help of Catherine de Medici of Italy. When she married King Henry of France, she put her own chefs and dessert makers in the palace. For more than one hundred years the recipes were a closely guarded secret.

THINK ABOUT WHAT IS IMPORTANT
This paragraph seems important because it tells how iced drinks and cold desserts were turned into ice cream. As I read, I wonder why ice cream recipes were kept secret.

GOING BEYOND THE READING

After reading an article, the good reader thinks about what he or she has learned. Here, the reader learned about how ice cream developed in the past. After reading this article, the reader might:

★ add some new words — like *savor* — to his or her continuing list of vocabulary words;

★ look at cookbooks for other interesting desserts;

★ go to the local library to take out books about ice cream; or

★ visit the local ice cream shop to sample some new flavors.

CHAPTER 2

TOOLS FOR UNDERSTANDING

By now, you have been reading for several years. Have you noticed that every year your reading skills have improved? You now enjoy reading stories and many other kinds of reading.

In order to read well and do well on tests, you need to have a good set of tools. This chapter focuses on two useful tools for both reading and writing:

Using "Question" Words

AND

Using Graphic Organizers

USING "QUESTION" WORDS

In the last chapter, you learned that good readers ask questions. When news reporters are sent to cover a story, they want to find out what is happening. Reporters learn what is taking place by asking six basic questions:

These words are known as the six **question words.** When you read a story or other type of reading, pretend you are a news reporter. Ask yourself as many of the six question words as you can:

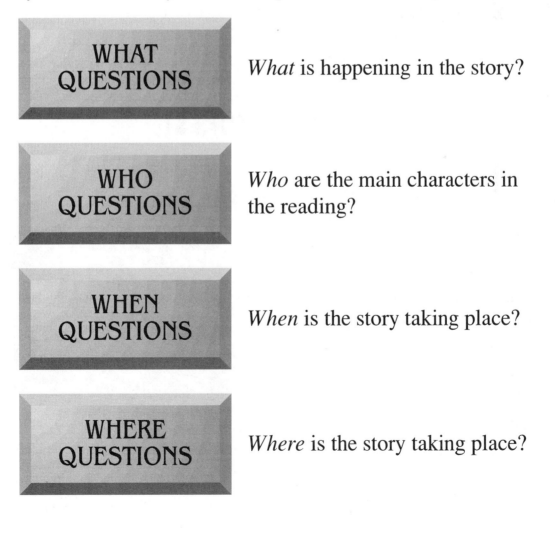

WHAT QUESTIONS — *What* is happening in the story?

WHO QUESTIONS — *Who* are the main characters in the reading?

WHEN QUESTIONS — *When* is the story taking place?

WHERE QUESTIONS — *Where* is the story taking place?

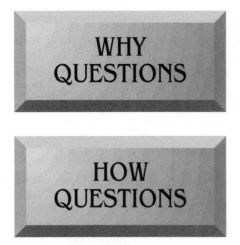

Why have the characters acted as they did?

How is this story going to end?

Whenever you read a story or other type of reading, think about these six question words. Answer these questions and you will better understand what you have read.

Read the passage below. It is the beginning of the book *The Courage of Sarah Noble* by Alice Dalgliesh. Answer as many questions as you can about the story by using the six question words.

NIGHT IN THE FOREST

Sarah lay on a quilt under a tree. The darkness was all around her, but through the branches she could see one bright star. It was comfortable to look at. The spring night was cold, and Sarah drew her warm cloak close. That was comfortable, too. She thought of how her mother had put it around her the day she and father started out on this long, hard journey.

CHECKING YOUR UNDERSTANDING

Now play the role of a news reporter. Write down as many questions about the story as you can. Use the six question words below as a guide. The first question word has been done for you.

WHAT?
- What did Sarah see through the branches?
- What did Sarah use to keep herself warm?

WHO?
- _____
- _____

WHEN?
- _____
- _____

WHERE?
- _____
- _____

WHY?
- _____
- _____

HOW?
- _____
- _____

USING GRAPHIC ORGANIZERS

Do you know what a graphic organizer is? A **graphic organizer** is a diagram that shows information. Often a graphic organizer uses circles, rectangles, and other shapes. These shapes are filled with important ideas and information. Sometimes, lines or arrows connect these shapes in order to show how one thing is related to another.

You can use a graphic organizer to picture information in a reading. Let's look at some of the ways graphic organizers help us to visualize information.

TOPIC OR WEB MAPS

One type of graphic organizer is a *topic* or *web map.* This is created by putting the topic or main idea of a reading in the center of the page. Then surround this topic or main idea with supporting facts and details. This type of graphic organizer is useful for a reading that *describes* an important idea, character, place, or event. Let's practice by reading the passage below. Then complete the topic map that follows.

THE HOUSE ON SANDLER'S LANE

Everyone in our community knew about the house at the end of Sandler's Lane. No one had lived in that dark, dreary house for more than a hundred years. Everyone knew that the house was haunted. Each Halloween, neighbors looked through the windows and swore they saw ghosts dancing inside the house. At other times of the year, people sometimes heard shrieks and other strange sounds coming from the house.

PRACTICE COMPLETING A TOPIC MAP

Directions: Fill in the blank boxes with details that help describe the house on Sandler's Lane.

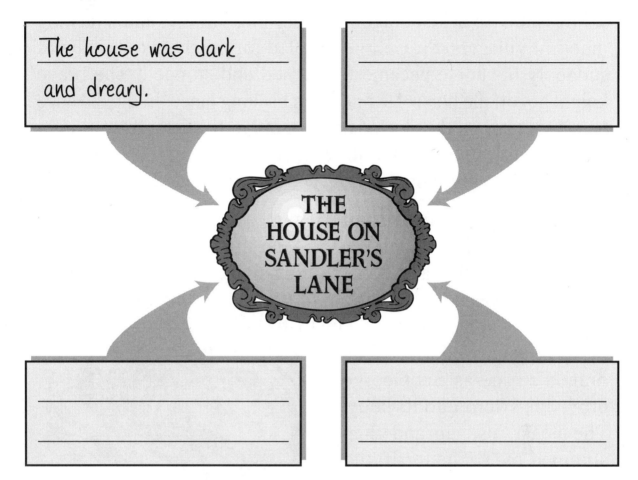

The house was dark and dreary.

THE HOUSE ON SANDLER'S LANE

SEQUENCE MAPS

Many stories and other readings tell about a series of events. A **sequence map** can help you see how these events are related. They show how events in a story move from one event to the next. To make a sequence map, make a box or circle for each event in the order that the event occurred. Then connect the events by arrows to show the passing of time.

Let's create a sequence map. First, read the story about a bold knight and a dragon. Then complete the sequence map that follows.

SIR GEORGE MEETS THE DRAGON

Sir George left his castle and set out on a very dangerous mission. A wicked dragon was burning villages and attacking innocent villagers. Sir George traveled for nearly two days, until suddenly his horse became frightened and stopped. The brave knight got off the horse. He put down his long lance. In the distance he saw a cave on the side of the mountain. Sir George could not see the monster, but he knew it was there. His nostrils filled with the smell of the dragon's fiery smoke, and his skin tingled from its heat.

Sir George, in full armor, began walking up the winding path that led to the dragon's cave. After the first turn, the dragon came into view. It was a bone-chilling sight. Taller than ten men, the dragon was covered with hard scales and breathed fire and smoke. Sir George ran straight up to the huge beast. An expression of surprise passed across the dragon's face as Sir George drove his sword into its body. The beast rose up and then slumped over. The terrifying dragon was dead!

PRACTICE COMPLETING A SEQUENCE MAP

Directions: Fill in the blank boxes on the following page to show the sequence of events in the story you just read. The first two boxes have been completed for you.

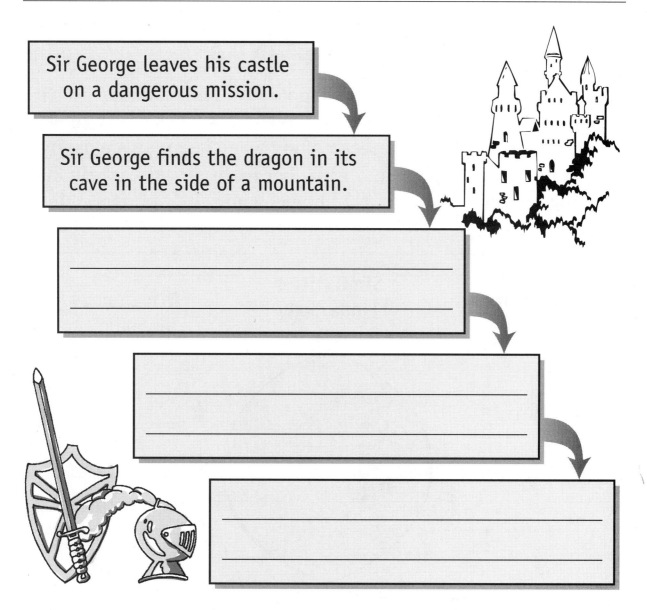

Sir George leaves his castle on a dangerous mission.

Sir George finds the dragon in its cave in the side of a mountain.

VENN DIAGRAMS

A **Venn diagram** is another type of graphic organizer. It is used to compare and contrast two items, topics, or concepts. To make a Venn diagram, draw two ovals or other shapes making sure the shapes overlap. In the overlapping area, write those things that the items have in common. In the parts of the ovals that do not overlap, write whatever is different about each item.

Now let's create a Venn diagram. First read the description that follows of Sally and Linda. Then complete the Venn diagram.

SALLY AND LINDA

Sally is the daughter of Linda. People say Linda and Sally have features that are alike. Both have brown eyes and a pretty smile. They both sing the same quiet melody whenever they are happy. But Sally likes to sleep late, while her mother rises early in the morning. Linda enjoys eating at home, while Sally prefers eating in a restaurant.

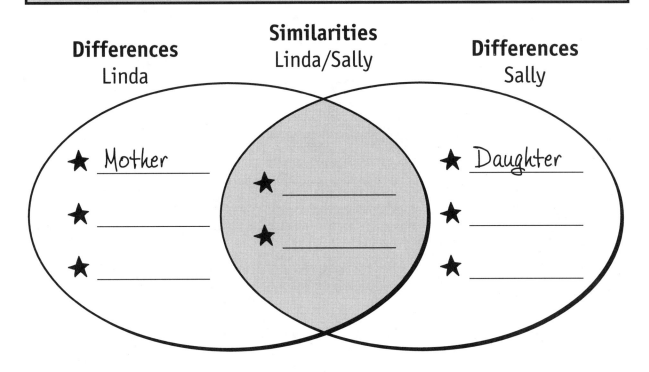

Differences
Linda

Similarities
Linda/Sally

Differences
Sally

★ Mother

★ Daughter

★ _____

★ _____

★ _____

★ _____

★ _____

★ _____

Remember: You can make Venn diagrams using any kind of shape, including circles and rectangles.

You should use these three kinds of graphic organizers — *topic maps, sequence maps,* and *Venn diagrams* — to help you as you read and to keep track of different kinds of information. By showing how ideas, facts, or events are related, these charts will help you understand them better. As you read the rest of this book, you will see how these different types of graphic organizers can be used.

CHAPTER 3

READING STORIES

There have been stories for as long as there have been people. The earliest stories were spoken. Story-tellers told or sang myths and legends to groups of listeners. Later, stories were written down. Stories help explain how things happen in the world. By telling stories, we share our experiences with others.

Many stories are make-believe. They are about imaginary people the story-teller has made up. Sometimes make-believe stories are about real people in make-believe situations. We call any writing about imaginary things **fiction.**

We read stories for enjoyment. Good stories help us to really stretch our imagination. They allow us to imagine what it would be like to live in faraway places or to have exciting adventures. We learn about other people's experiences and lives. Stories also put us in touch with all kinds of emotions. They can make us laugh or cry. They can make our hearts pound with excitement.

THE PARTS OF A STORY

Do you have a favorite story? Why is it your favorite? What makes it such fun to read? Just as the recipe for a great dessert will contain many ingredients, so too does a good story.

If your favorite story is like most stories, it will have four main ingredients:

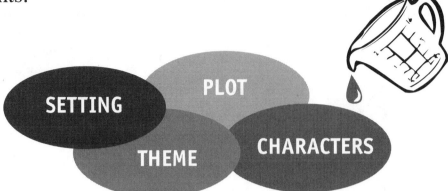

Do you know what each of these ingredients is? Let's look at a well-known story from ancient Greece to see how they blend together. As you read, remember to use the strategies of good readers — *ask yourself questions, create mental images,* and *make predictions.* Use the sheet that immediately follows the story to record your thoughts.

THE GOLDEN TOUCH

Long ago, in ancient Greece, a king named Midas spent much of his day eating and listening to music. One day, his gardener brought an old man to see him.

Midas immediately recognized that the old man was Silenus. Midas knew Silenus was a close friend of Dionysus — the god of merry-making.

For ten days and nights, Midas entertained Silenus. Midas then brought Silenus back to Dionysus. Because Midas had entertained his friend Silenus, Dionysus was very happy.

CONTINUED ▶

THE STORY SETTING

The story setting is **when** and **where** the story takes place. Often the setting is described at the beginning of the story. Sometimes, the author gives clues to indicate the story's time and place. You must examine the clues in the story to figure out the time and place.

A story setting can be in the past, present, or future, or even in an imaginary world where time hardly seems to exist. Fairy tales often begin with "Once upon a time …" to indicate an imaginary setting. A long story may even have more than one setting. As you read, try to create *mental images* of where the story takes place.

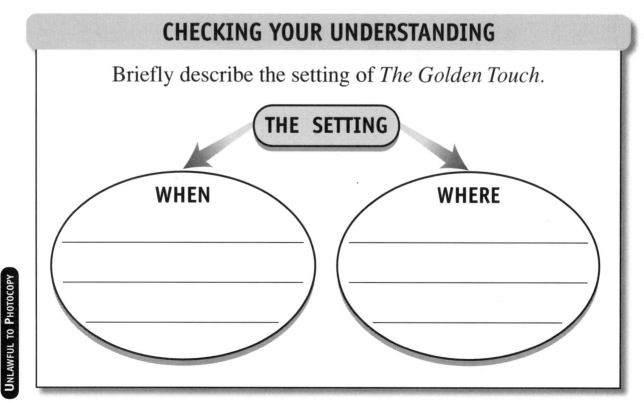

CHECKING YOUR UNDERSTANDING

Briefly describe the setting of *The Golden Touch*.

THE SETTING

WHEN

_____
_____
_____

WHERE

_____
_____
_____

THE STORY CHARACTERS

The characters of a story are *who* the story is about. Characters can be imaginary people or real people in an imaginary setting. Story characters may even be animals or objects that act like people. In **fables,** a special type of story, the main characters are often animals.

Most stories have only one or two main characters. Although a story may have several other characters, these other characters are less important.

The story is mostly about the main characters and their adventures. Readers identify with the main characters by imagining what it would be like to be them. Sometimes the author will describe what a character is like by drawing a picture of that character with words. At other times, you have to figure out what the characters are like by the way they act and what they do in the story.

When reading or listening to a story, you should ask yourself the following questions about the characters:

★ What do they look like?

★ How do they act?

★ What do they think and feel?

★ How do they change as the story develops?

CHECKING YOUR UNDERSTANDING

List the characters in *The Golden Touch*.

(1) _____   **(3)** _____

(2) _____   **(4)** _____

Who is the main character of the story? _____

Complete a topic map describing the main character of the story.

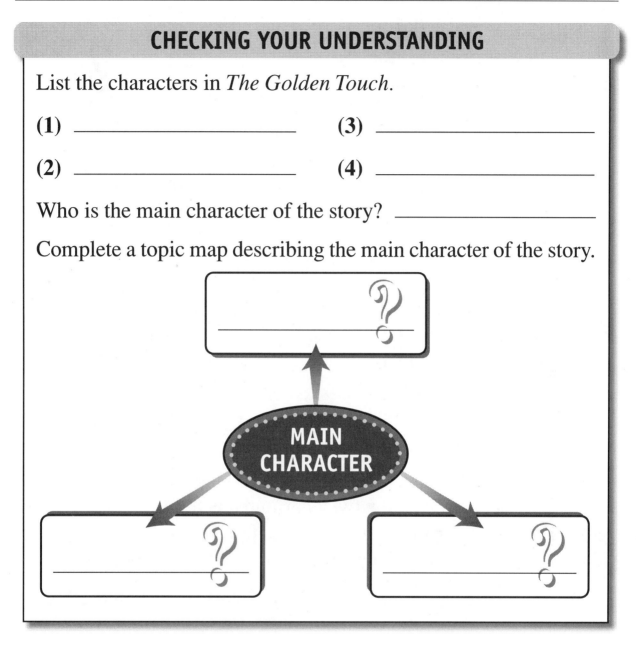

THE STORY PLOT

The plot is ***what happens*** in the story. In most stories, the main characters face one or more problems. Sometimes a character wants to do something that is difficult, like climb a mountain or win a race. At other times, the main character has a conflict with another character in the story. For example, two boys may be competing with each other for the top prize in a contest.

The **plot** is the series of events that unfold in the story. As these events take place, the characters try to solve or overcome the main problem they face in the story. As you read or listen to a story, try to focus on the *most important* events in the plot.

An author often tries to maintain the reader's interest by creating some kind of excitement and suspense. The reader wants to continue reading the story to find out what happens.

As the plot unfolds, new twists or unexpected turns often occur, making the main problem worse. Eventually, the main characters think of a way to solve their problems or learn to accept them.

When you are reading or listening to a story, you should ask these questions about the plot:

 What problems do the main characters face?

 What events in the story affect these problems?

 What actions do the characters take to deal with these problems?

 Are the problems finally solved? If so, how are they solved?

CHECKING YOUR UNDERSTANDING

It often helps to make a sequence map to follow the plot of a story. Complete the sequence map below for *The Golden Touch*. Only include the most important events. The first two events have been completed for you:

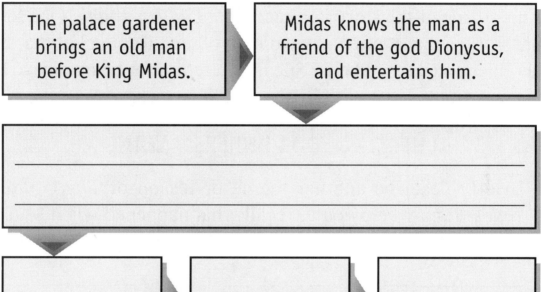

The palace gardener brings an old man before King Midas.

Midas knows the man as a friend of the god Dionysus, and entertains him.

Another way you can make a sequence map is by drawing pictures. Pretend you are creating a comic book of the story, *The Golden Touch*. Make a comic strip showing the main events. Remember, it is *not* your artistic ability that is important, but how well you show the story. Use a separate sheet of paper to create your comic strip.

THE STORY THEME OR LESSON

Stories usually teach us a message or lesson we can use in our own lives. This *message* or *lesson* is often called the **theme** of the story. Some stories have more than one theme. Themes show and tell us about life and human nature.

This is true of the story you read, *The Golden Touch*. One lesson of that story is that it often pays to help others. Remember that King Midas entertained the old man Silenus. In return for being nice to him, Midas was granted one wish by the god Dionysus.

CHECKING YOUR UNDERSTANDING

1. Briefly describe another theme or lesson of *The Golden Touch*. It may help you to recall what happened when Midas got his wish.

_____

_____

_____

_____

2. In what way does a theme of the story remind you of something that has happened in your own life or that you have read or learned about? Explain.

_____

_____

_____

POEMS

Another type of literature is poetry. Some poems are like stories. They have a setting, characters, a plot, and a theme. However, not all poems tell a story. Some poems simply describe something — such as a beautiful garden or the arrival of winter.

THE CHARACTERISTICS OF POETRY

Most poems have a common characteristic. They use word pictures and the sounds of words to help express their meaning.

★ **Rhythm.** When you read a poem, the words are usually arranged so that you can hear a strong beat. It is almost like reading to the beat of a drum.

★ **Rhyme.** Many poems are written so that a word or line ends in the same last sound as another word or line. This is known as *rhyme*.

★ **Other Sound Patterns.** Poets use other sound patterns to give poetry a musical quality. For example, they may use a series of words that begin with the same sound, like "<u>s</u>oft as <u>s</u>kin."

★ **Imagery.** Poets use images or word pictures to express ideas. Poets also try to appeal to our other senses.

ANALYZING POETRY

The first thing to ask yourself when reading a poem is whether the poem *tells a story* or *describes something*. If the poem is telling a story, you should keep track of all the story elements, just like any other story. For other poems, you should identify what the poet is describing and the poet's feelings about it.

Let's look at a poem. Instead of full sentences, poetry is often organized by lines. In a poem, the reader usually pauses at the end of each line. Several lines of poetry are organized into paragraphs known as **stanzas.** The poem *City* has two stanzas.

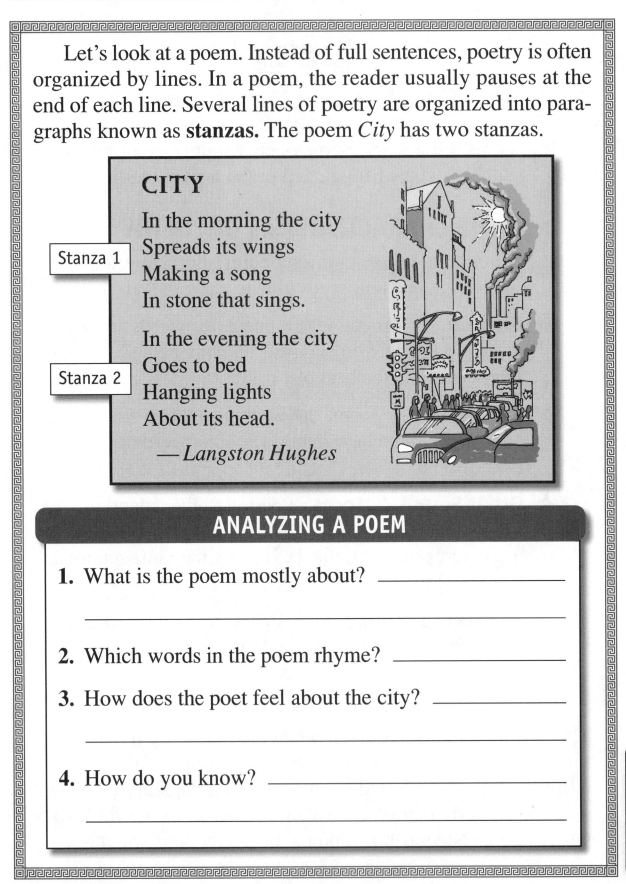

CITY

Stanza 1	In the morning the city Spreads its wings Making a song In stone that sings.
Stanza 2	In the evening the city Goes to bed Hanging lights About its head.

—Langston Hughes

ANALYZING A POEM

1. What is the poem mostly about? _____

   _____

2. Which words in the poem rhyme? _____

3. How does the poet feel about the city? _____

   _____

4. How do you know? _____

   _____

Practice Exercises

Directions: Read the story below by Pleasant DeSpain. Then complete the graphic organizer that follows:

OLD JOE AND THE CARPENTER

Old Joe lived in the country by himself. His best friend was his closest neighbor. They had grown old together. Their wives had died, and their children were grown and had moved away. All they had left were their farms and each other.

For the first time in their long relationship, they had a disagreement. It was a silly argument over a stray calf that neither one of them really needed. The calf was found on the neighbor's land and he claimed it.

Old Joe said, "No, that calf has the same marking as one of my cows, and it belongs to me!"

They were stubborn men, and neither would give in. Rather than hit each other, they stopped talking. They stomped off to their respective homes. Two weeks went by without a word between them.

One Saturday morning, Old Joe heard a knock on his door. He was surprised to find a young man who called himself a "carpenter" standing on his porch. He had a toolbox at his feet, and there was kindness in his eyes. "I'm looking for work," he explained. "If you have a project, I'd like to help out."

CONTINUED →

Old Joe replied, "As a matter of fact, I do have a job for you. See that house there? It's my neighbor's. You see that creek along our property line? That creek wasn't there last week. He did that to spite me! He dug that creek-bed from the pond right down the property line and then flooded it. Now that creek separates us. I'm so mad at him! I've got lumber in my barn and everything you'll need to build a tall fence all along that creek. Then I won't have to see his place any more. That'll teach him!"

The carpenter smiled and said, "I will do a good job for you, Joe."

The old man had to go to town for supplies. He got on his wagon and left. The young carpenter carried the lumber from the barn to the creek and started to work. He measured, sawed, and nailed the boards into place all day without stopping. With the setting of the sun, he went to put his tools away. He was finished.

Old Joe pulled up, his wagon filled with supplies. When he saw what the carpenter had built, he couldn't speak. It wasn't a fence, but a beautiful footbridge that reached from one side of the creek to another.

Just then, Old Joe's neighbor crossed the bridge, his hand stuck out, and said, "I'm sorry about our argument, Joe. The calf is yours, I just want us to be friends."

"You keep the calf," Old Joe said. "I want us to be friends, too. The bridge was this young fellow's idea. And I am glad he did it."

One way to understand what you have read is to make a graphic organizer. On the page below is one type of organizer often used for stories. Complete the organizer based on the story you just read:

STORY MAPPING

TITLE: _____

SETTING: _____

★ **Where:** _____

★ **When:** _____

MAIN CHARACTERS:

★ **Who:** _____

★ **Who:** _____

★ **Who:** _____

PLOT: *(List the events in the order that they happened)*

❶ _____

❷ _____

❸ _____

❹ _____

❺ _____

THEME OR LESSON: _____

_____

CHAPTER 4

READING FOR INFORMATION

We read for a variety of reasons. Sometimes we read imaginary stories for fun and pleasure. At other times, we read to find out information and to learn new things.

TYPES OF INFORMATIONAL READINGS

Informational readings, called **non-fiction,** are about real people, places, events, and things. They come in a wide variety of forms.

★ **Articles.** Articles are short informational pieces that are usually read in one sitting. You can find articles in newspapers, magazines, and encyclopedias. They tell you the basic facts about something. Let's examine a typical article from a newspaper.

Mapletown News

LIGHTNING STRIKES HOUSE ON TAYLOR STREET

At 11:30 p.m. last night, a home on Taylor Street was hit by lighting during a violent thunderstorm. No one was injured.

Mr. Jones, owner of the home at 42 Taylor Street said, "We were all asleep when we were suddenly awakened by this very loud noise."

The purpose of an article is generally to tell a reader the *who, what, when, where, why,* and *how* of something. *Does this article tell the reader something about each of these question words?*

★ **Essays.** An **essay** gives an author's opinions and feelings about a single topic or issue. Let's look at an essay about cats.

THIS MAN'S BEST FRIEND — CATS

Of all the world's creatures, I have to admit that I admire cats the most. Ever since I was a young boy growing up in Minnesota, there was just something about the sleek bodies, pointed ears, whiskers, and eyes of cats that inspired instant love in me. When a cat gently purrs and rubs its body against my leg, it establishes a place of love in my heart.

In this essay, the author gives his feelings about cats and their impact on his life.
How does the author feel about cats?

★ **Biography / Autobiography.** A **biography** is an article or book written by someone about a person's life and accomplishments. An **autobiography** is an article or book in which someone writes about his or her own life.

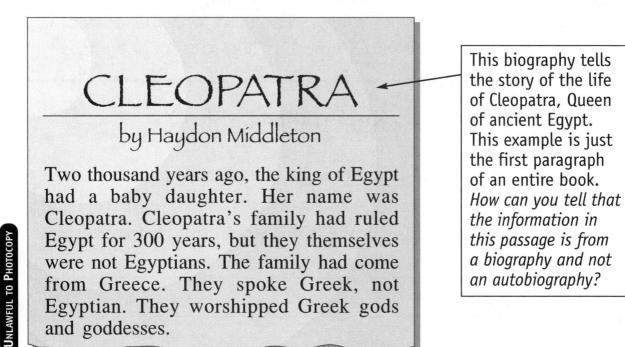

CLEOPATRA

by Haydon Middleton

Two thousand years ago, the king of Egypt had a baby daughter. Her name was Cleopatra. Cleopatra's family had ruled Egypt for 300 years, but they themselves were not Egyptians. The family had come from Greece. They spoke Greek, not Egyptian. They worshipped Greek gods and goddesses.

This biography tells the story of the life of Cleopatra, Queen of ancient Egypt. This example is just the first paragraph of an entire book.
How can you tell that the information in this passage is from a biography and not an autobiography?

All of these types of readings have something in common. They give information about a topic. The title and the first paragraph of each reading usually identifies the topic of the reading. The **topic** is the subject of the reading — what it is mostly about.

> **The following passage is the beginning of a longer article. Read the passage. Then identify the topic of the article.**

TREASURE HUNTER
by Ellen Hobart

Inch by inch, wiggle by wiggle, something down there is moving. It creeps along the sandy ocean floor. It moves past the swaying seaweed and around the rusty anchor chain.

It's the carrier snail, and it's hunting for treasure. Right now, it might be looking for a small skinny shell. Later on, it might choose a smooth speckled stone or a jagged piece of coral. The snail is always searching for the perfect piece to add to its collection.

CHECKING YOUR UNDERSTANDING

1. What is the topic of this article? _____

2. What are some things you would expect to learn from this

article? _____

_____

THE PARTS OF AN INFORMATIONAL READING

Just as stories have different parts, so do informational readings. There are two major parts to an informational reading:

The MAIN Idea

SUPPORTING DETAILS

Do you know how each part works? Let's look at a short informational reading. As you read this passage, remember to use the strategies of good readers — *ask questions, create mental images,* and *make predictions.* Use the data sheet that follows to record your thoughts.

ABRAHAM LINCOLN

Abraham Lincoln was one of our greatest Presidents. When he was elected in 1860, slavery was permitted in much of the United States. Southern states feared Lincoln would end slavery. They tried to set up their own separate country. Lincoln led Americans into the Civil War to reunite the country. He bravely kept fighting despite many battlefield losses. Victory in the war finally reunited the country and ended slavery.

Library of Congress

Abraham Lincoln

You may wish to look back at this reading about Abraham Lincoln as you answer the following questions:

BEING AN ACTIVE READER

1. What did you already know about the subject of the reading?

_____

_____

2. What information in the reading did you find interesting?

_____

_____

3. What questions did you have about the reading?

_____

_____

_____

4. What did you think was important in the reading?

_____

_____

5. What new words or phrases from the reading would you like to make a part of your everyday vocabulary?

_____

_____

THE MAIN IDEA OF A READING

The general point that an author makes about the topic of a reading is known as the **main idea.** For example, an author may show you that the subject of a biography was a very good person by telling you about her good deeds. Or the author may show that a place is very dangerous by pointing out the dangers experienced by visitors to it.

Remember, the *main idea* is not any particular detail. It describes what the reading is about *as a whole.* It is the most important thing in the reading. Even an imaginary story may have a main idea.

FINDING THE MAIN IDEA

When you read something for information, you can take two steps to find the main idea.

> ## STEP 1:
> Decide the topic of the reading.

Determine the general subject of the reading. Is it about a person, place, or event? Think of the topic as an umbrella. It should be large enough to cover everything discussed in the reading. For example, the topic of the reading on page 35 was **Abraham Lincoln.**

> ## STEP 2:
> See what the writer is saying overall about the topic.

Once you have decided on the topic, focus on what the writer has to say about it. Look for an overall message about the topic.

This message is the author's main idea. Other details in the reading should explain or support the main idea.

Sometimes a special sentence in the reading will identify the main idea. Often it is at the beginning or end of the reading. Sometimes the main idea is unstated. The reader has to figure it out from the details.

In the paragraph on Abraham Lincoln the main idea was that he was one of our nation's greatest Presidents. The specific facts mentioned in the reading help to support this main idea.

CHECKING YOUR UNDERSTANDING

Identifying the Main Idea. Here is a list of points made in an informational reading. Check (✔) the one point that states the main idea of the informational reading.

❑ Apples are good for the lungs.

❑ Blueberries help to slow down the body's aging process.

❑ Eating fruit helps to keep the body healthy.

❑ Oranges provide the body with Vitamin C.

Explain your choice: _____

_____

As you learned in this chapter, the *topic* and *main idea* of an informational reading are often identified *early* in the reading. The author tells readers what he or she is writing about.

You can also check the *end* of the reading. Sometimes, the conclusion will summarize the main idea and the most important details in the passage. Also examine the title, subheadings, and illustration captions for clues to the main idea.

THE SUPPORTING DETAILS

To help the reader understand the main idea or to show the reader that the main idea is correct, an author supplies examples, details, and illustrations. Each of these helps to support the author's main idea. It is through the use of these details and examples that the author explains the main idea and tries to show that it is correct.

CHECKING YOUR UNDERSTANDING

What were some of the details used by the writer to support the idea that Abraham Lincoln was a great President?

★ _____

_____

★ _____

_____

★ _____

_____

CHANGING WHAT YOU HAVE READ INTO A GRAPHIC ORGANIZER

It is sometimes easier to understand the main idea and supporting details of a reading by looking at a graphic organizer. You learned about graphic organizers in **Chapter 2.** Let's see how the paragraph about Abraham Lincoln might be turned into a graphic organizer. Does this diagram help you see the relationship between the main idea and supporting details?

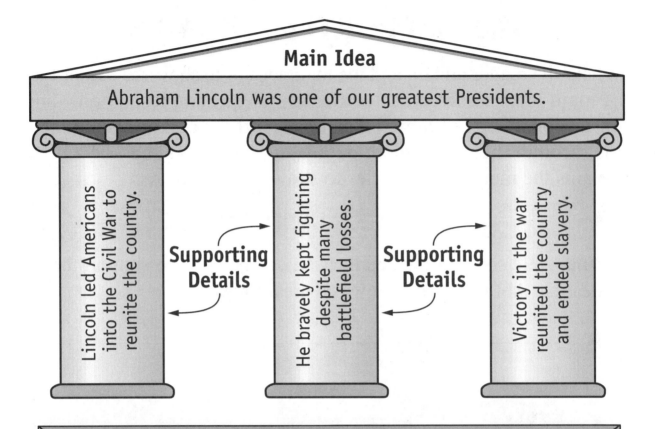

Main Idea

Abraham Lincoln was one of our greatest Presidents.

Lincoln led Americans into the Civil War to reunite the country.

Supporting Details

He bravely kept fighting despite many battlefield losses.

Supporting Details

Victory in the war reunited the country and ended slavery.

SUMMARY

In <u>Chapters 3 and 4</u>, you learned about two different types of readings. Remember that what you find in a reading will depend largely on the type of reading it is.

IN A STORY

In a story, you can expect to find a <u>setting</u>, <u>characters</u>, and a <u>plot</u>. In addition, you can also expect to find one or more story <u>themes</u>.

IN AN INFORMATIONAL READING

In an informational reading, you can expect to find a <u>topic</u>, a <u>main idea</u> about that topic, and <u>supporting details</u>. Supporting details may include descriptions, facts, and examples.

Practice Exercises

Directions: Read the following article by Ellen Hobart. Then identify the topic, main idea, and the supporting details or examples.

Animals often have special ways of protecting themselves from enemies. Many animals use their color to help keep them safe. No one has to teach them. It is one of nature's built-in protections. The brown sparrow looks like part of the nest it sits upon. The winter coats of some jackrabbits match the color of the snow. The spotted fish blends in with the pebbles of the mountain stream that it swims in.

CHECKING YOUR UNDERSTANDING

1. What is the *topic* of this paragraph? _____

2. What is the *main idea* of this paragraph? _____

_____

3. List *three* supporting details from the paragraph:

★ _____

★ _____

★ _____

Directions: Read the following article about a young African American's experiences at West Point — a college which cadets attend to become officers in the U.S. Army. Then identify the *main idea* and the most important *supporting details* in a graphic organizer.

THE STORY OF HENRY FLIPPER
by Bea Bragg

As the West Point ferry docked, seventeen-year old Henry Flipper, a young African American, tugged at his shirtsleeves. *How will I do at the U.S. Military Academy at West Point?*

Henry was born of slave parents in 1856 in Georgia. Until the Civil War, African Americans in the South were kept in slavery. Even after the Civil War, African Americans often faced prejudice.

After the war ended in 1865, Henry received an education in schools run by Northern sympathizers. He was confident his teachers had prepared him well. He was not so confident about how he would put up with the insults that other black men had received there. Would he have to fight back and lose everything he had dreamed of — becoming an engineer and becoming a proud soldier?

As Henry walked past the barracks on his first day, cadets leaned from windows, teasing and jeering him. Henry, who was more than six feet tall, pulled himself up, looked straight ahead, and walked on.

Henry faced isolation and loneliness at West Point, but did well academically. He had never felt such joy as when he successfully completed all of his exams. "I was so happy. The other cadets shook my hand. All signs of prejudice were gone."

CONTINUED ➞

On June 14, 1877 graduates received their diplomas. When Henry's name was called, a roar went up from the audience. The roar drowned out the pounding in Henry's ears. They were applauding him. Fellow cadets crowded around him to shake his hand.

Henry was the first black graduate of West Point. He was assigned to Fort Sill in Oklahoma. At this post, he received praise for designing a ditch that drained water from the area, eliminating malaria — a serious health problem.

Student cadets practice marching at West Point.

Henry was happy at Fort Sill. Things changed when he was transferred to Fort Davis in Texas. There, a superior officer charged him with stealing and "conduct unbecoming an officer and a gentleman." Henry was cleared of the stealing charge but was dismissed from the army. He was broken-hearted. For the rest of his life, he tried to have his dismissal reversed.

Henry went on to become a famous engineer, whose skill gained him national and international fame. He also served as a newspaper editor, translator, scholar, writer, and historian.

Henry Flipper died in 1940 at the age of 84. Forty years later the army cleared his name. In 1978, his remains were taken from a grave in Atlanta and moved to his home town. He was reburied with full military honors.

CONTINUED ▶

In 1977, one hundred years after Henry's graduation, an award in his name was established at West Point. It was to be given to "the cadet who demonstrated the highest qualities of leadership and determination in the face of unusual difficulties." Henry Flipper would have been so proud!

Now that you have completed reading the article, fill in the graphic organizer below. It has already been started for you.

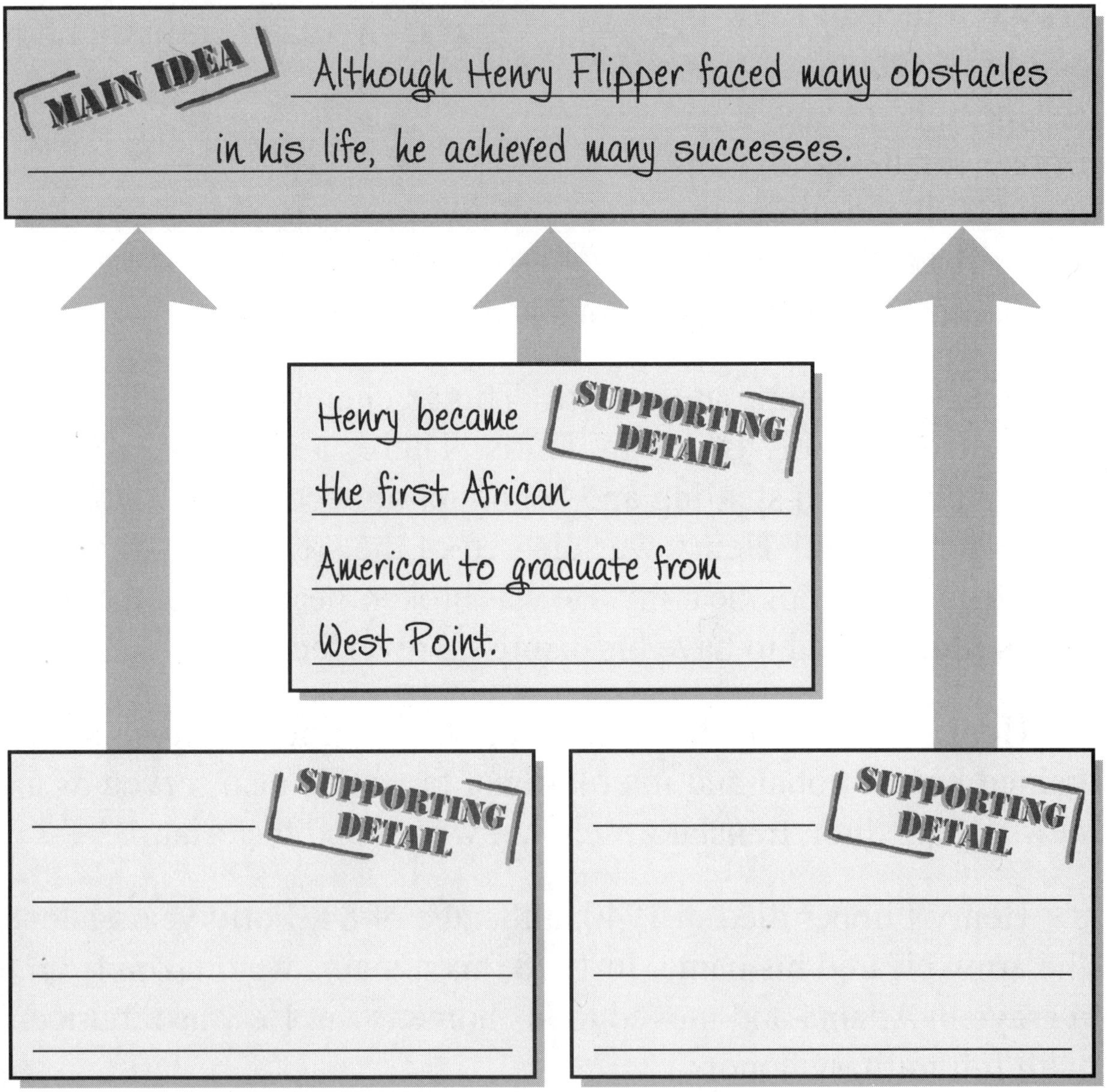

MAIN IDEA   Although Henry Flipper faced many obstacles in his life, he achieved many successes.

SUPPORTING DETAIL   Henry became the first African American to graduate from West Point.

SUPPORTING DETAIL

SUPPORTING DETAIL

CHAPTER 5

ANSWERING MULTIPLE-CHOICE QUESTIONS: OPENING IMPRESSIONS

Do you know what a multiple-choice question is? A **multiple-choice question** is a question followed by several possible answers. Your job is to pick the choice that best answers the question. Here is an example:

---

1. **How many hours are there in one day?**
   A 7 hours
   B 12 hours
   C 24 hours
   D 48 hours

The answer is "C." There are 24 hours in a day. The other choices are wrong. Notice that you would *not write 24 hours* to answer the question. Instead, you should use the letter — "C" — to answer the question.

You may be asked to take a test to show your reading ability. A reading test asks you to read one or more passages. Each passage is followed by several questions. Many of the questions about the reading passage will usually be multiple-choice questions. This and the next several chapters will give you practice in answering different kinds of multiple-choice questions.

There are five main types of multiple-choice questions about a reading. Each type of question focuses on a different step of the reading process:

1. Get a general impression of what the reading is about

2. Figure out the meaning of unfamiliar words or phrases

3. Focus on details in the reading — *who, what, when,* and *where*

4. See how details are connected — think about *how* and *why*

5. See how details in the reading connect to a *main idea* or *theme*

In a sense, questions about a reading are arranged as if you were approaching the reading from a distance.

★ At first, you can see only roughly what the reading is about. You get a first impression about the reading.

★ Then you look at the reading more closely. You start to see the different parts of the reading passage. You start to focus on those parts and how they are connected.

★ When you are done looking at the parts, you step back again to view the reading as a whole (*to see what the whole reading is about*).

Multiple-choice questions test your ability to understand the reading at each of these steps.

WHAT THE READING IS MOSTLY ABOUT

On a reading test, one of the first questions you are likely to see will ask for your general impression of the reading. It will ask you what the reading is *mostly about.* This type of multiple-choice question will usually appear as: *What is the reading passage mostly about?* Or the question might ask: *What would be the best title for this reading?*

To answer this kind of multiple-choice question, first read the passage carefully. Then think about what you have read. What was the *most important* information in the reading?

★ **A Story.** In a story, think about the main characters, the central problem, and the most important events in the story. Try to make a sentence in your head that summarizes what happened in the story. For example, *The Golden Touch* was about a king who turned everything he touched into gold and then found he could not survive that way.

★ **An Informational Reading.** In an informational reading, the question asks you about the *topic* of the reading. For example, you may read an article telling what meteors are made of, how fast they travel, and how many meteorites fall to the Earth each year. The topic of this article is meteors.

Remember that the *topic* of an informational reading will often be stated at the beginning of the passage. Look at the title and any sub-headings in the reading for clues. At other times, the topic will not be stated. Use details in the reading to figure it out. Ask yourself — *what do the details in this reading have in common?*

After you form a general impression of the reading, look over the answer choices. Select the answer that best summarizes what the whole reading is about. Choices that focus on individual details rather than the whole story or reading are probably not the correct answers.

If you are not sure which answer is best, review the passage a second time by **skimming.** To skim, read the passage over quickly to get a general sense of what it is all about.

Let's practice answering a question that asks what an informational reading is *mostly about*. Read the passage below. Then answer the question that follows.

It looks easy! Glancing around a Chinese or Japanese restaurant, you see diners using chopsticks with ease. But when *you* try handling the long wooden utensils, one chopstick crosses over the other, and your food plops back onto your plate. In desperation, you spike a shrimp with the pointed end of a chopstick. The food makes it to your mouth. But to the Japanese, what you just did is as rude as eating peas with a knife.

Why did anyone ever think eating with wooden sticks was a good idea? Well, it was better than eating with your fingers, which is what most people did five thousand years ago.

A Chinese story explains that once, a hungry person couldn't wait for his food to cool. He grabbed a couple of sticks, and pulled out a piece of meat. The others copied him. The use of chopsticks soon spread to other Asian countries and reached Japan by about 500 A.D.

1. What would be the best title for this reading selection?
  A Restaurant Food   **C** Dining in Japan
  B The Story of Chopsticks   **D** A Hungry Person

CHECKING YOUR UNDERSTANDING

What is the answer to **Question 1**? _____ Explain your answer.

_____

Now let's practice answering an *opening impression question* about a story. Read the story. Then answer the question that follows.

A lion slept in the forest. A mouse ran across the lion's nose. Awakened, the lion grabbed the tiny creature. The poor mouse begged, "Please, please, spare me. Let me go and one day I'll repay you." The lion was amused to think a mouse could ever help him. Being a generous lion, he let the mouse go.

Some days later, the lion was caught in a hunter's net. Unable to free himself, the lion roared angrily. The mouse knew his voice and ran to help the lion. Jumping onto the ropes of the hunter's net, the little mouse began to chew at them. Before long the lion was free. "You laughed when I said I would repay you," said the mouse. "Now you see that even a little mouse can help a huge lion."

2. **What is the story mostly about?**
   A   A little mouse who is almost eaten by a lion.
   B   A little mouse who can eat through rope.
   C   A huge lion who is awakened by a little mouse.
   D   A little mouse who repays a lion's kindness.

The best answer to this question is "**D.**" The story is about a lion who allows a mouse to go free and is later saved by that mouse. The other choices are true, but they deal with only one part of the story.

Practice Exercises

The laundry room in the back of my house is small and painted green. The door to the laundry room is made of frosted glass. This laundry room has always reminded me of Grandma. I saw her only once or twice a year because she lived in California.

My favorite memory of Grandma was when she visited me in New York City. She took me to see a Broadway show. After the show, we waited for the subway train home. Somehow I got lost and was left on the subway platform. I remember yelling for grandmother and seeing her pink hat as she silently screamed to me behind the glass doors of that green subway car. I remember the train as it flew past me in a blur. When we were later reunited, I was so happy at being found. Grandma was so upset she was crying. That was the first time I felt connected to this woman I called Grandma.

Now as I stand in the laundry room I remember her wrinkled face and white hair. I look at the frosted glass that I can never quite see through, just like the train's windows. And as I look around the laundry room, I am reminded of the woman who showed me her love that day.

1. **Which of these sentences best describes the passage?**
   A This is a story of a grandmother who grows old.
   B This is a story about a young girl's laundry room.
   C This is story about a girl's memories of her grandmother.
   D This is a story about how frightening it is to get lost.

CHAPTER 6

VOCABULARY QUESTIONS

After you have a general idea of what a reading is about, the next step is to make sure you understand any hard words in the reading. *Vocabulary questions* test your understanding of how a word or phrase is used in a passage. Such questions test your ability to understand unfamiliar words or to understand the use of words that have several meanings. Let's look at a passage with an unfamiliar word.

> Jack was new in the neighborhood and decided to take a walk. During his stroll, Jack passed an old, dilapidated house on Mill Road. The windows of the house were broken, the roof appeared to leak, and no one had lived there for over twenty years.

1. **In this passage, "Jack passed an old, dilapidated house on Mill Road." What does *dilapidated* mean in this sentence?**
   A just built
   B very crowded
   C made of stone
   D run down

CHECKING YOUR UNDERSTANDING

What is the answer to **Question 1**? _____ Explain your answer.

_____

_____

The best answer is "**D.**" How could you answer this even if you did not know the meaning of the word *dilapidated*? Often, good readers come across words they do not know. However, a good reader uses a variety of methods to figure out the meaning of a strange word.

This chapter will give you some new ways to figure out the meaning of unfamiliar words and phrases. You can use these techniques to help you answer *vocabulary questions* on tests. You should also work to improve your vocabulary as you read. Look up words in the dictionary when you do not know their meaning. Get in the habit of keeping a "word list" of important new words you learn.

USE CONTEXT CLUES

Suppose you sound out a word but still do not know what the word means. The next step in figuring out the meaning of an unfamiliar word is to look at surrounding words and sentences. These surrounding words and sentences often provide clues about the meaning of a word or phrase. The clues that surround a word or phrase are called **context clues.**

Sometimes the sentence or surrounding sentences will actually give you the definition. For example, read the following sentence:

> John saw Ms. Jones, the *superintendent*, who was in charge of all three of the town's elementary schools.

CHECKING YOUR UNDERSTANDING

What does the word *superintendent* mean? _____

What context clue provides the hint? _____

_____

At other times, context clues may tell you what the unfamiliar word or phrase *is not*. Again, read the following sentence:

> Unlike the *idle* Mr. Adams, Ms. Smith busy every day.

CHECKING YOUR UNDERSTANDING

What does the word *idle* mean? _____

What context clue provides the hint? _____

_____

Often you will have to find clues throughout the passage to figure out the meaning of the unfamiliar word. Read the following passage:

The athlete was *mammoth* in size. He was nearly seven feet tall. His arms were thicker than many people's legs. With his powerful and muscular arms, he could easily lift a car off the ground or throw a baseball out of the stadium.

CHECKING YOUR UNDERSTANDING

What does the word *mammoth* mean? _____

What context clues provide the hint? _____

_____

You could easily see the *irritated* expression on Jack's face at hearing the news. Jack was looking forward to seeing a movie with his mother. Just last week his mother had promised him they would go to the mall to see the new Disney movie. Now his mother had changed her mind. Instead, they would go shopping in the mall for school clothes.

CHECKING YOUR UNDERSTANDING

What does the word *irritated* mean? _____

What context clue provides the hint? _____

_____

When you come across an unfamiliar word or phrase in a reading passage, think of yourself as a detective. Use context clues to figure out the meaning of the word or phrase. Let's summarize what we have just learned about using context clues:

 Look at the other words in the sentence.

 Read a few sentences *__before__* and *__after__* the sentence in which the unfamiliar word or phrase appears.

 Based on the rest of the sentence and on neighboring sentences, try to guess the meaning of the word or phrase.

It may help to think of an unfamiliar word or phrase as an empty box. Based on what you read in the surrounding sentences, what word or words would you expect to find in that empty box?

In the cold climate of Scotland, many people enjoy hot ▢ *for breakfast. They make their breakfast by boiling ground oats in hot water or milk.*

What words do you think might fit in the box?

- _____
- _____

USE YOUR KNOWLEDGE OF PARTS OF SPEECH

When you come across an unfamiliar word, it also helps if you can discover its part of speech. Most often, the unfamiliar word will be a *noun, verb, adjective,* or *adverb.*

★ A **noun** is a person, place, or thing.
For example: ***Jack*** likes to play tennis.

★ A **verb** is an *action* or *being* word — it tells what nouns do or what is being done to them.
For example: He ***ate*** too much, and now he ***felt*** sick.

★ An **adjective** describes a noun.
For example: I just bought a ***silver*** car.

★ An **adverb** describes a verb, adjective, or another adverb.
For example: He ran very ***swiftly.***

Read the sentences below. After you read them, fill in the *part of speech* that belongs in each blank box.

- ☐ is a very pretty girl.

- Tiffany ☐ her dinner.

- My mother bought a shiny, ☐ car.

Once you know the part of speech, it is easier to think of other words you might use in place of the unfamiliar word. The word you use to replace the difficult word should be the same part of speech.

USE WORD ANALYSIS

Another way to figure out the meaning of an unfamiliar word is to break it down into its parts. You can then see if any of these parts reminds you of other words you already know.

First say the word silently to yourself. Think if you have ever heard that word before. Then divide the word into syllables. Each **syllable** is a word or part of a word that is pronounced with a single vowel sound. Some words have many syllables, such as *lol • li • pop.* Other words have one syllable like *hat.* If you read the word *hatrack* and divide it into syllables, you can guess it's something to hang a hat on.

PREFIXES, ROOTS, AND SUFFIXES

Recognizing the syllables of a word can sometimes help you to break down a word into smaller parts: *prefix, root,* and *suffix.* For example, let's look at the word *unbreakable.*

ROOTS

Any word can serve as a **root.** The root is the basic word. Prefixes and suffixes are added to it. In the word *unbreakable, break* is the **root.**

PREFIX

A **prefix** is a syllable or group of syllables that is added in front of the root to change its meaning. In the word *unbreakable,* *un* is the **prefix.**

Here are some common *prefixes* you may see while reading.

Prefix	Meaning	Examples
re	again	*re*view, *re*write, *re*do
un	not	*un*happy, *un*healthy
mis	incorrectly	*mis*spell, *mis*lead

Some prefixes can be confusing since they may have more than one meaning. For example, *in* can either mean *inside* (*in*doors) or *not* (*in*correct).

SUFFIX

A **suffix** is a syllable or group of syllables added to the end of a word. In the word *unbreakable,* *able* is the **suffix.** Now let's examine some common suffixes you will frequently see while reading.

Suffix	Meaning	Examples
ful	full of something	care*ful*, hope*ful*, trust*ful*
able	able to do something	break*able*, depend*able*
ness	state of being something	kind*ness*, happi*ness*, sad*ness*
er	person who does something	teach*er*, work*er*, carpent*er*

When we analyze the word *unbreakable,* here is what we see:

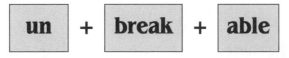

unbreakable = not able to be broken

COMPOUND WORDS

A **compound word** is made up of two separate words that are added together to form a new word.

| home | + | work | = **homework** |

By breaking up a compound word into its parts, you can often figure out what the word means. Try the examples that follow:

Word	What two words make up the compound word?	What does this word mean?
bodyguard	_____ + _____	
courtroom	_____ + _____	
everything	_____ + _____	

If you break a difficult word into its parts, it can often help you to figure out its meaning. Remember that some prefixes and suffixes have more than one meaning.

APPLYING WHAT YOU HAVE LEARNED

You should use *word analysis* together with *context clues* and *parts of speech* to help you figure out the meaning of an unfamiliar word.

❑ Examine surrounding words and sentences for context clues.

❑ Figure out the part of speech of the unfamiliar word.

❑ Use word analysis by:
  • breaking the word into syllables
  • checking the word for familiar prefixes, roots, and suffixes
  • breaking up compound words into parts

To answer multiple-choice questions on unfamiliar words and phrases, first look at the context clues. Try to figure out the part of speech and use word analysis. Then, look at the different answer choices. Substitute each of the choices for the unfamiliar word or phrase. Read the sentence silently to yourself using each choice. Pick the one choice that makes the most sense.

A powerful eagle seized a small lamb in her talons, and flew off with it to her nest. A nearby crow was watching and decided to copy the eagle. The crow swooped down and grabbed a large sheep. However, when the crow tried to fly away, it could not lift the sheep. Unlike the eagle, the crow's claws were not as strong. A nearby shepherd saw the crow and guessed what had happened. He caught the crow. That evening the shepherd gave the crow to his children. "What do you call it?" they asked. He replied, "This is a crow. But if you ask him, *he* would say he's an eagle."

2. **In the phrase, "A powerful eagle seized a small lamb in her talons," What does the word *talons* mean?**
   A wings   **C** stomach
   B claws   **D** eyes

CHECKING YOUR UNDERSTANDING

What is the answer to **Question 2**? _____ What clues helped you to figure out the meaning of the word *talons*? _____

_____

When you read, make a list of important *new* words. This will help you improve your vocabulary. Some vocabulary questions may simply test your knowledge of words that students in your grade should know. This type of question might ask you to select a word that is **similar** or **opposite** to a particular word or to choose the correct definition of the word. The question may be without context clues since you are expected to know the meaning of the word already. If the word is in a sentence, pick the choice that makes the most sense if it is substituted into the sentence. You can practice this type of question by answering the following questions:

3. **A *cloak* means the same as a** _____ .
   A pillow
   B blanket
   C hat
   D coat

4. **Someone who is a *colonel* is** _____ .
   A an officer in the army
   B the leader of a country
   C the manager of a business
   D the captain of a ship

5. **What does *display* mean?**
   A to show something
   B to hide something
   C to behave badly
   D to practice an instrument

6. **What is the OPPOSITE of *collapse*?**
   A to rise up
   B to hide something
   C to behave badly
   D to practice an instrument

> The teacher was very *patient* in helping the student.

7. **Which sentence uses the word *patient* in the same way as the sentence in the box above?**
   A The doctor still had one patient in the waiting room.
   B Sylvia did not mind waiting because she was patient.
   C The swim coach was always patient in giving advice.
   D It's hard to be patient when you are in a hurry.

8. **To boast is to**
   A cook on a fire
   B run away
   C brag
   D glow in the dark

> Both teams thought the referee was very *fair*.

9. **Which sentence uses the word *fair* in the same way as the sentence in the box above?**
   A On Wednesdays, they go to the town fair.
   B The judge's decision in the trial was quite fair.
   C The boy had green eyes and fair hair.
   D We enjoy going on the rides at the county fair.

> He was quite handsome with a very *deep* voice.

10. **Which sentence uses the word *deep* in the same way as the sentence in the box above?**
    A Juan is a deep thinker.
    B The hole in the ground was quite deep.
    C He dug deep into his pocket and came up with a quarter.
    D The striking of the bell made a deep sound.

Practice Exercise

Directions: Read the story and answer the *vocabulary questions* that follow.

BELLING THE CAT

The mice called a meeting to decide on *a course of action* to free themselves from their enemy, the cat. They wanted to find some way of knowing when the cat was coming, to give them time to run away. The mice lived in such *trepidation* that they hardly dared stir from their dens by night or day.

Many plans were discussed at the meeting. However, none of them were thought to be good enough.

At last a young mouse in the room got up and said, "I have a plan that seems very simple, but I know it will be successful. All we need to do is to hang a bell around the cat's neck. When we hear the bell ringing, we'll know that the cat is coming."

All of the mice were surprised that they had not thought of such a simple plan before.

But *in the midst* of their rejoicing an old mouse arose and said. "I agree that the plan of the young mouse in the back of the room is very good. But let me ask one question during all of this celebrating and rejoicing: *"Which of us will put the bell on the cat?"*

1. **The mice met to "decide on a course of action to free them-selves from their enemy, the cat." What does** *a course of action* **mean?**

   A a plan to do something   **C** a way to punish a cat
   B how to join forces with a cat   **D** how to get more food

   What is the answer to **Question 1**? _____ Which clues

   helped you to figure out the meaning of the phrase? _____

   _____

2. **"The mice lived in such** *trepidation* **that they hardly dared stir from their dens by night or day." What does the word** *trepidation* **mean?**

   A bravery   **C** debt
   B fear   **D** pain

   What is the answer to **Question 2**? _____ Which clues

   helped you to figure out the meaning of the word? _____

   _____

3. **"In the midst of their rejoicing, an old mouse arose." What does the phrase** *in the midst* **mean?**

   A at the start   **C** at the end
   B in the middle   **D** a foggy moment

   What is the answer to **Question 3**? _____ Which clues

   helped you to figure out the meaning of the phrase? _____

   _____

CHAPTER 7

QUESTIONS ABOUT DETAILS IN A READING

In this chapter, you will learn how to answer questions that test your understanding of details in a reading. *Detail questions* focus on the **who, what, when,** and **where.**

Detail questions about a **story** usually ask for details about the story's setting, characters, and events. To the right are some of the ways the question may appear:

★ What is a character like?

★ What does a character do?

★ When does the story take place?

★ Where does the story take place?

Detail questions about an **informational reading** usually ask about important supporting details and facts. Following are some ways questions may appear:

★ What are particular things in the reading like?

★ When did events in the reading occur?

★ Where did events in the reading take place?

★ Which facts support the author's viewpoint?

SCANNING TO FIND ANSWERS

The answer to a *detail question* will most often be found directly in the reading. If you do not immediately recall the answer to the question, you should scan the reading.

To **scan** is to look quickly through the text for specific information. One way to scan is to look for *key words*. For example, if a question asks about a character's job in the story, look for places in the reading where the character's name is mentioned. Force your eyes to race along the page. Stop each time you see the name of the character. Each time you stop, check the sentence to see if it mentions the character's job. If it does not, continue to scan the reading.

You may recall that in a previous chapter you learned about **skimming.** Although both *skimming* and *scanning* require you to read through a passage quickly, there are important differences:

HOW SKIMMING AND SCANNING DIFFER

★ **Skimming.** When you skim, you read through a passage quickly *to get a general idea* of what the reading is all about. Use the title, subheadings, and captions under pictures as clues.

★ **Scanning.** When you scan, you read through a passage quickly *to locate specific information.* Once you locate the information, read that sentence or section more carefully.

Sometimes the answer to a *detail question* will not be found directly in the passage. Instead you will have to figure out the answer by using information from two or more places in the passage. You will learn more about using your thinking skills to answer such questions in a later chapter.

Let's practice answering *detail questions*. Read the passage below. Then answer the questions that follow. The passage is adapted from the first chapter of a novel, *Half Magic*, by Edward Eager.

HOW IT BEGAN

1   It began one day in summer about thirty years ago, and it happened to four children.

2   Jane was the oldest and Mark was the only boy, and between them they ran everything.

3   Katherine was the middle girl, of a mild disposition and a comfort to her mother.

4   She knew she was a comfort, and easy-going, because she'd heard her mother say so.

5   And the others knew she was, too, by now, because ever since that day Katherine would keep boasting about what a comfort and how easy-going she was.

6   Finally, Jane declared she would utter a piercing shriek and fall over dead if she heard another word about it.

7   Martha was the youngest, and very difficult.

Now answer the following questions about the passage.

1. What time of year does this story begin?
   A winter
   B fall
   C spring
   D summer

> If you do not recall the answer to this question immediately, *scan* the passage. Look for some mention of one of the four seasons of the year.

CHECKING YOUR UNDERSTANDING

What is the answer to **Question 1**? _____ The first sentence states, "It began one day in *summer* about thirty years ago, and it happened to four children." Therefore, the answer is "**D**" — the story begins in summer.

2. **Who was the youngest child?**
   A Jane
   B Mark
   C Martha
   D Katherine

CHECKING YOUR UNDERSTANDING

What is the answer to **Question 2**? _____ In which sentence

did you find the answer? _____

_____

3. **Which is the best description of Katherine?**
   A She had a mild disposition.
   B She never boasted.
   C She made piercing shrieks.
   D She was very difficult.

CHECKING YOUR UNDERSTANDING

What is the answer to **Question 3**? _____ In which sentence

did you find the answer? _____

_____

4. How did Katherine know she was a comfort to her mother?

   A She felt she was very helpful.

   B She heard her mother say so.

   C Her little sister told her.

   D Her father told her.

CHECKING YOUR UNDERSTANDING

What is the answer to **Question 4**? _____ In which sentence did you find the answer? _____

5. How did Jane feel about Katherine's repeating that she was a comfort to her mother?

   A It made Jane happy to hear it.

   B Jane did not like Katherine's boasting.

   C It gave Jane a mild disposition.

   D Jane began to boast that she and Mark ran everything.

CHECKING YOUR UNDERSTANDING

What is the answer to **Question 5**? _____ To answer this question, you need to apply your reasoning powers to information in the story. The passage does not directly tell you how Jane felt about Katherine's boasting. It does tell you that Jane said she would utter a "piercing shriek" if Katherine boasted another time. From this reaction we can figure out that Jane disliked Katherine's boasting.

FACT AND OPINION QUESTIONS

Do you know the difference between a *fact* and an *opinion*? Some detail questions may ask you to identify a fact or an opinion.

FACT

A **fact** is a statement that can be shown to be correct or true. "The table is red" is a statement of fact. People can look at the table to see if it is red. Other facts can be checked by using other sources. Assume someone tells you that there was a fire yesterday at 42 Maple Lane. You can look in the newspaper, call the fire department, or even visit Maple Lane to check if there really was a fire.

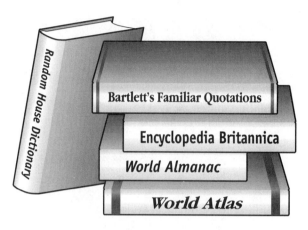

OPINION

An **opinion** is a statement of personal feelings or beliefs. Words such as *think, feel, probably,* and *believe* often show that a statement is an opinion. This statement is an opinion: "I believe George Washington was our greatest President." No one can prove that Washington was our greatest President. The statement just tells us the speaker's personal opinion.

Sometimes writers make statements that look like facts but which are actually opinions. Ask yourself: is this a fact that can be checked or just an expression of the writer's feelings or beliefs?

Let's practice answering a *fact and opinion question*. Read the passage from "The Wandering Continent" by Eon Bilokur. Then answer the question.

Alfred Wegener was a curious man. He looked at the sky and wondered about the weather. He looked at the ocean and wondered what was under it. And when he looked at a map of the Earth, he wondered if it had always been the same. One day in 1911, Wegener came upon some books that showed the locations of fossils found around the world. Until then no one had proven why fossils of certain animals, like dinosaurs and snails, are found on lands so far apart. The animals were unable to swim across the ocean. Some scientists wondered if land "bridges" once connected the lands. Others thought that, if the continents were once part of a giant land mass, animals could have walked across before the land split up. Wegener became convinced that this was what had happened.

6. **Which of the following expresses an opinion about Wegener?**
   A He was a curious man.
   B He read some books showing fossil locations in 1911.
   C Fossils of the same animals have been found on lands far apart.
   D He believed separate areas were once part of a giant land mass.

CHECKING YOUR UNDERSTANDING

What is the answer to **Question 6**? _____ Explain your answer.

_____

Practice Exercises

Directions: This article tells about life in ancient Egypt. Read the article. Then answer the questions that follow.

PASS THE BREAD, PLEASE
by Cyndy Hall

What did children eat in ancient Egypt? Did their parents make them finish their vegetables before dessert? Did kids have peanut butter and jelly sandwiches 4,000 years ago?

No one knows for sure if kids in ancient Egypt had to eat all their vegetables. But there are clues in the ruins of tombs that answer a lot of questions.

Families in ancient Egypt grew their own food. They planted beans, onions, cucumbers, and other crops. Farmers often took heads of "sacred lettuce" to temples to thank the gods for a good harvest. Fruit trees were every-where. Children picked dates and figs for snacks.

The world's first beekeepers were Egyptians. Hives were kept in large pottery jars. Beekeepers simply brushed the bees aside to collect their honeycombs. The honey was stored in containers. Children must have enjoyed dipping their fingers in these bowls for a sweet treat.

Perhaps they put honey on their bread, too. Children ate bread at every meal. Bread was ancient Egypt's main food. There were hundreds of kinds of breads, in different shapes and sizes. Some recipes used fruits, garlic, or nuts to flavor the loaves.

CONTINUED →

Eating bread caused some problems. Bits of desert sand and stones often got into the dough. Archaeologists have discovered that most Egyptian mummies have worn and missing teeth. They believe the Egyptians wore their teeth down while chewing on their bread.

So what did Egyptian children eat instead of peanut butter and jelly sandwiches? It's a recipe you'll probably not want to try at home. Children cut thick slabs of bread, spread garlic on top, and then piled on raw onions. Yummy? Maybe that's why they chewed mint leaves to sweeten their breath!

1. **What vegetable did ancient Egyptians take to their temples to thank their gods for a good harvest?**
   A cucumbers
   B beans
   C lettuce
   D onions

2. **What was the main food of most ancient Egyptians?**
   A honey
   B beans
   C fruits
   D bread

3. **Which shows that Egyptians had some problems eating bread?**
   A Mummies had worn teeth.
   B Children used garlic.
   C Lettuce was left in temples.
   D Children ate dates and figs.

4. **What did ancient Egyptian children eat instead of peanut butter and jelly sandwiches?**
   A garlic and onion sandwiches
   B bread and honey sandwiches
   C mint leaf sandwiches
   D bean and onion sandwiches

CHAPTER 8

QUESTIONS ABOUT CONNECTING DETAILS

Once you master the individual details of a reading, you can begin to make connections between these details. Connecting details allows you to follow a series of events, explain why things happen, make comparisons, or draw conclusions from the reading. To make these connections, you have to apply your reasoning powers to what you have read. Your understanding and knowledge will help you to make these connections.

Some multiple-choice questions will test your ability to make connections among details. This chapter examines five types of questions that focus on connecting the details in a reading. They are:

Connecting the Details

1. SEQUENCE

Sequence questions look at the order in which things happen.

EXPLANATION

Explanation questions ask why things happen.

2. 3. COMPARE-AND-CONTRAST

Compare-and-contrast questions compare details in the reading.

PULLING-IT-TOGETHER

Pulling-it-together questions test your ability to draw conclusions from story details.

4. 5. PREDICTION

Prediction questions ask you to apply what you've read to new situations.

SEQUENCE QUESTIONS

Sequence questions test your ability to follow events in a story or in an informational reading. For a *sequence question,* the answer can usually be found directly in the reading passage.

A writer will usually present events in the order in which they happened. Look for clue words to help you decide the sequence of events. These clue words include: **after, before, then, since, next, last,** and **first.** Look for hints about a change of time or season that may take place in the story. Let's practice answering a *sequence question.* Read the passage below. Then answer the questions that follow.

There once lived a farmer who owned the most wonderful goose. Every day, the goose laid a beautiful golden egg for him. The farmer sold each egg at the market. Soon he became very rich. But the farmer was impatient with the goose. It was giving him only one egg a day. He felt he was not getting rich fast enough. One day, he came up with an idea to get all the golden eggs at once. He decided he would cut the goose open and take out all the eggs. The farmer killed the poor goose. But when he opened it up, not a single golden egg was inside. And now his precious goose lay dead.

1. **Which event in the story occurred first?**
   A The farmer killed the goose.
   B The goose laid a golden egg each day.
   C The farmer decided to cut the goose open.
   D The farmer became very rich.

CHECKING YOUR UNDERSTANDING

What is the answer to **Question 1**? _____ What is the correct

sequence of events in the story? _____

_____

---

2. **Which event happened last?**
   A The farmer sold an egg each day at the market.
   B The farmer became impatient with the goose.
   C The farmer opened up the goose but found no eggs.
   D The farmer decided to kill the goose.

CHECKING YOUR UNDERSTANDING

What is the answer to **Question 2**? _____ Explain your choice.

_____

_____

EXPLANATION QUESTIONS

When we read about events, we often think about *why* these things happened. An *explanation question* tests your understanding of cause-and-effect relationships.

★ The **cause** of something is what made it happen. For example, if you turn the switch of a light, you make it go on. The cause of the light's going on is your turn of the switch. Questions asking for the cause of something often begin with the question word *why.*

★ The **effect** of something is what happens as a result. The effect of your turning on the light switch is that the light goes on.

Sometimes an event will have many causes and several effects. You can use a topic or sequence map to show *causes* and their *effects*. Use arrows to indicate cause-and-effect relationships. For example,

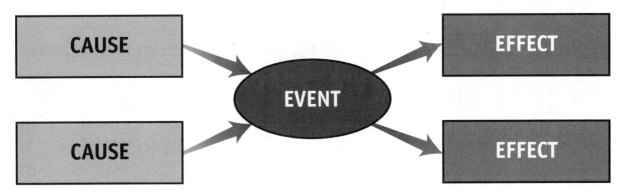

You should look for the answers to *explanation questions* in the reading itself. Often, clue words will alert you. Key words include: *why, because, as a result,* and *due to.* Sometimes you will not find these words in the reading, but it will still be clear that one event in the reading caused another. If the question asks *why* something happened, look through the passage to see the reasons why it occurred.

Quite often you will find that something happens in a story or in real life because of the actions of a character or a real-life person. Think about why the character acted as he or she did. What did the character want to achieve? The *reason why* a character or person did something may help to explain why it happened. Always remember to think about the motives of the characters when answering an *explanation question.*

Let's practice answering an *explanation question*. Read the following passage. Then answer the questions that follow.

An African chief had three sons. Each was talented in fighting and riding. Each son competed with his brothers to be the best. One day the chief decided to settle their constant arguing. He announced he would test his sons to see who had the greatest skills.

The chief pointed to a tree next to their home. "I'll use this tree to test which of you is most talented," said the chief. The sons quickly mounted their horses. They rode off a distance and stopped.

The eldest son raced his horse toward the tree. He thrust his spear through the tree and rode through the hole he had made. The second son raced his horse forward. When he reached the tree, he and his horse leaped over it.

The youngest son went last. He rode forward, grabbed the tree and pulled it out, roots and all. He rode on, waving the tree over his head. Thrilled by this deed, the chief considered his youngest son to be the greatest one.

3. **Why did the chief decide to hold a contest among his sons?**
   A to see which son he loved the most
   B to see if his sons were truly loyal to him
   C to see who had the greatest skills
   D to see who would become the next chief

CHECKING YOUR UNDERSTANDING

What is the answer to **Question 3**? _____ Explain your answer.

_____

_____

4. Why did the youngest son pull the tree out of the ground?

   A He wanted to show he was more clever than his brothers.

   B He wanted to show how much he loved his mother.

   C He wanted to show he was angry with his father.

   D He wanted to show his strength and skill.

CHECKING YOUR UNDERSTANDING

What is the answer to **Question 4**? _____ Explain your answer.

_____

_____

_____

COMPARE-AND-CONTRAST QUESTIONS

Sometimes we compare things to understand them better. We want to know how they are different and how they are similar. A multiple-choice question may ask you to compare two *characters*, two *places*, or two *events*. You have to figure out how they are alike and how they are different. You may even be asked to compare the same character at different moments in the story.

The answer to a *compare-and-contrast question* is often found directly in the reading. Scan the passage until you can find where one or both of the things or people you are comparing can be found. Make a mental note about the features of each item. Then think about how the two items are similar and how they are different.

In **Chapter 2,** you learned to compare two items by using a Venn diagram. If time permits, it helps to write down the main similarities and differences in the form of a Venn diagram. Then you can answer the question more easily.

Let's practice answering a *compare-and-contrast question*. Read the following passage. Then answer the questions that follow.

Darrell and José were schoolmates. They were traveling together through the forest when suddenly a huge bear jumped out of the brush. Darrell, thinking of his own safety, climbed up a tree. José threw himself on the ground. He lay still, as if he were dead. José knew that bears will not touch a dead body. The bear sniffed at José's head awhile and then walked away. After the bear left, Darrell climbed down from the tree. He said, "It looked to me as if that bear whispered in your ear. What did he say?"

José answered coldly, "He said it's unwise to have a friend who runs away when you most need him."

5. In what way were Darrell and José ALIKE?

   A They enjoyed fighting bears.

   B They liked climbing trees.

   C They went to the same school.

   D They always helped each other.

CHECKING YOUR UNDERSTANDING

What is the answer to **Question 5**? _____ Explain your answer.

_____

_____

_____

6. How did José's feelings about Darrell change after they met the bear?

   A José became less trusting of Darrell.

   B José grew jealous of Darrell.

   C José refused to talk to Darrell ever again.

   D José grew closer to Darrell as a friend.

CHECKING YOUR UNDERSTANDING

What is the answer to **Question 6**? _____ Explain your answer.

_____

_____

_____

"PULLING-IT-TOGETHER" QUESTIONS

"Pulling-it-together" questions test your ability to draw conclusions from details in the reading. They call for you to apply your own reasoning powers. To answer a *"pulling-it-together" question,* use details in the reading as clues. Then apply your own thinking skills to identify the best answer.

For example, a *"pulling-it-together" question* might ask you to select a conclusion based on a series of facts in an informational reading:

In the early 1800s, American pioneers settled the area around the Great Lakes. In order to survive, these pioneers had to cut down trees, plant fields with crops, and build their homes. A typical pioneer family worked from early morning until nightfall. Men would clear the land and plant the fields. At the same time, women helped with the farm animals, cooked, made clothes, and cared for the children.

7. **What conclusion can be made about the lifestyles of American pioneers in the early 1800s?**
   A Most pioneers came from the Northeast.
   B The pioneers were concerned about protecting nature.
   C Pioneer women worked just as hard as men.
   D The pioneers did not have any farm animals.

The answer is "**C.**" Although the passage does not compare the work of pioneer men and women, it lists the jobs each filled. It also explains that pioneers had to work from early morning until nightfall. From this, you can *draw the conclusion* that pioneer women worked just as hard as men.

Let's practice answering a *"pulling-it-together" question.* Read the following passage.

Jerusalem is an ancient city in the Middle East. Today, it is located in the country of Israel. Palestinians, a group of Arabs in Israel, want to have their own country. They want Jerusalem to become their capital. Israeli Jews and Palestinian Arabs both consider Jerusalem to be a very holy city.

8. **What conclusion can be drawn from this passage?**
   A Most Israelis and Palestinians are friends.
   B Israelis and Palestinians disagree about the future of Jerusalem.
   C Jerusalem should continue to remain in Israel.
   D Jerusalem should become the capital of Palestine.

CHECKING YOUR UNDERSTANDING

What is the answer to **Question 8**? _____ Explain your answer.

_____

_____

PREDICTION QUESTIONS

After you have completed a reading, you should connect what you have learned with what you already know. *Prediction questions* test your ability to apply what you have learned from the reading to new situations. *Prediction questions* might appear as follows:

★ If the story could continue, what might happen next?

★ What might a character in the story do in a different situation?

To answer a *prediction question,* apply what you have learned in the story to the new situation. For example, you may read a story about a woman who was generous with her money. A *prediction question* might ask what would happen if she met a starving stranger. We could predict that the woman would try to help the person in need.

Let's practice answering a *prediction question.* Read the passage below. Then answer the question that follows.

By 1871, about 300,000 people lived in Chicago. Most lived and worked in buildings made of wood. Sidewalks and many streets were made of wooden blocks. The summer and fall of 1871 were extremely dry. It hardly rained for months. Dry wooden buildings, lumberyards and grain storehouses were ready to ignite. On Sunday night, October 8th, a fire started in Mrs. O'Leary's barn in the city's center. Other wooden buildings quickly caught fire. The pumping house also burned, leaving Chicago's fire departments without water. The city burned for two days. About 300 Chicagoans died. More than 18,000 buildings were destroyed, and nearly 100,000 people were left homeless.

9. **Based on the reading, what action would you predict Chicagoans to have taken following the Great Fire of 1871?**

   A People rebuilt Chicago using mostly wood.

   B New laws required buildings to be made of fireproof materials.

   C Chicago closed down its fire department.

   D Most people moved out of Chicago.

CHECKING YOUR UNDERSTANDING

What is the answer to **Question 8**? _____ Explain your choice.

_____

Practice Exercises

Directions: Read the story below. Answer the questions that follow.

DAMON AND PYTHIAS

Damon and Pythias had been best friends since childhood. They trusted each other like brothers, each knowing the other would do anything for his friend.

The King of Syracuse grew annoyed when he heard about a speech Pythias was giving. Pythias was telling people that no man should have unlimited power. In a rage, the king summoned Pythias and his friend Damon. "Who do you think you are, spreading trouble among the people?" the king demanded.

"I spread only the truth," Pythias answered. "There can be nothing wrong with that."

CONTINUED

"And do you say that the king's laws are not good? This talk is treason," the king shouted. "Take back what you said or you'll face trouble." Pythias refused to take back anything he had said.

"Then you'll die," said the king. "Do you have any last requests?" Pythias asked the king to let him go home to put his house in order. The king laughed. "Do you think I'm stupid? If I let you leave the city, you will never return." Pythias said he would give the king a pledge.

"What pledge could you possibly give to make me think you'll ever return?" the king demanded.

At that instant Damon stepped forward. "I will be his pledge," he said. "Keep me here as your prisoner, until he returns. For sure Pythias will return so long as you hold me."

The king said, "Very well, but if you're willing to take your friend's place, you must also accept his punishment. If Pythias doesn't return, you'll die in his place." Damon replied that he had no doubt that Pythias would keep his word.

Pythias was set free, while Damon was put in prison. After several days, the king visited Damon to see if he was sorry he had made the bargain. "Time is almost up," the king said. "You're a fool to rely on a friend's promise. Did you think he would sacrifice his life for yours?"

CONTINUED ▶

"He has been delayed," Damon answered. "He'll be here on time. I am as confident of this as I am of my own existence." The king was startled at his confidence, and left Damon in his cell.

The fatal day arrived. Damon was led before the executioner. The king greeted him with a smile. "It seems your friend failed to turn up," he laughed. "What do you think of him now?"

"He is my friend," Damon answered. "I trust him."

Just as he said this, Pythias staggered in, bruised and battered from exhaustion. He rushed to his friend. "You are safe," he gasped.

"My ship was wrecked in a storm, and then bandits attacked me on the road. But I refused to give up. I have come back to receive my punishment." The king heard his words with amazement. It was impossible to resist the power of such friendship.

"The sentence is cancelled," he declared. "I never believed such loyalty could exist in a friendship. You've shown me I was wrong. You shall be rewarded with your freedom. I ask only one favor."

"What is that?" the two friends asked.

The king answered, "Teach me how to be such a loyal friend."

1. **Which event in the story happened first?**
   A In a rage, the king summoned Damon and Pythias.
   B Pythias returned to save his friend.
   C Pythias asked the king to let him go home.
   D The king visited Damon in prison.

   Sequence

2. **What happened after Damon said he would take the place of his friend Pythias?**
   A The king agreed to let Pythias go home.
   B The king immediately set Pythias free.
   C The king had Damon arrested for speaking out.
   D The king refused to let Pythias leave for home.

   Sequence

3. **Why did the King of Syracuse have Pythias arrested?**
   A He was a ruler who arrested people for no reason.
   B He was jealous of the relationship between Pythias and Damon.
   C He was angry at a speech Pythias had given.
   D He feared a plot to overthrow him.

   Explanation

4. **What caused Damon to volunteer as a stand-in for Pythias?**
   A Pythias owed Damon a favor.
   B They were very good friends.
   C Damon wanted Pythias to continue making speeches.
   D Damon knew the king was afraid to execute Pythias.

   Explanation

5. **What effect did the return of Pythias have on the king?**
   A The king ruled that Damon and Pythias could no longer be friends.
   B The king had both men arrested.
   C The king wanted to learn how to become a loyal friend.
   D The king was angered when he found that Pythias had returned.

   Explanation

6. **What was one way in which Damon and Pythias were ALIKE?**
   A They both spoke out against the king.
   B They were the same age.
   C They were willing to betray each other if necessary.
   D They were willing to sacrifice their
      lives for each other.

   Compare-and-Contrast

7. **Which term best describes the character of Pythias?**
   A loyal
   B foolish
   C incapable
   D cowardly

   Pulling-It-Together

8. **If Pythias had failed to return, how might this story have ended?**
   A The king would have set Damon free.
   B Damon would have tried to escape from prison.
   C The king would have executed Damon.
   D The king would have become good friends
      with Pythias.

   Prediction

9. **If Damon had been arrested instead of Pythias, how would Pythias have behaved?**
   A He also would have volunteered to take his friend's place.
   B He would have turned against Damon.
   C He would have fled the city.
   D He would have helped the king imprison Damon.

   Prediction

CHAPTER 9

QUESTIONS ON THE MAIN IDEA OR THEME

In **Chapter 5,** you learned about questions that test your general impression of a reading. In later chapters, you learned about questions that test your understanding of details in the reading. After you have carefully read all the details, you should mentally step back from the reading passage and ask yourself:

> ## What was the message or main idea of this reading?

The details in the reading passage should help you to do more than just tell what the reading is mostly about. They should help you to understand the author's *main idea* or *theme*.

You have already learned that every informational reading has a **main idea.** The main idea is the message that the author is trying to communicate. It is the most important information in the reading. The rest of the reading gives details that support or explain the main idea.

A person who writes a story also usually has a message. However, in a story the message is not usually called the main idea. Instead, the main message of the author is called the ***theme*** of the story. A story can have more than one message or theme. Each one is the lesson that the story teaches.

FINDING THE MAIN IDEA OF AN INFORMATIONAL READING

Think of the main idea as a newspaper headline. In one short sentence or phrase, a headline summarizes what the entire story says.

Read the following paragraph. Then write a headline that expresses its main idea.

Marco Polo was born in Venice in 1254. In those days most people did not travel far from their homes. Marco was only 17 years old when his father and uncle, two wealthy Italian merchants, decided to take him along on their travels.

Marco traveled thousands of miles with them. They passed through the mountains and deserts of Turkey, Persia, and Afghanistan. The journey took more than three years. Marco was twenty years old when they finally reached the empire of China. Few Europeans had even heard of China at that time.

*Marco Polo
arrives in China*

Now, write a headline expressing the main idea of this reading. Remember, the main idea tells about the whole passage, not just specific details.

Someone who reads your headline should have a good idea of what the passage says:

A multiple-choice question may ask you about the main idea. Such questions can appear in many different ways:

★ What is the ***main idea*** of the passage?

★ Which sentence ***best summarizes*** what the author is saying?

All of these questions have *one thing* in common. They test your understanding of what you have read. They all ask you for the ***main idea*** of the passage.

To answer a *main idea question* about an informational reading, first think about the topic of the reading. Then think about the author's message on that topic. Sometimes the author may state the main idea in a single sentence. At other times, you will have to figure out the main idea. Think of a single sentence that sums up the passage and what the author is writing about.

Next, look at the answer choices. Select the answer that *best summarizes* what the whole reading is about. Choices that focus only on specific details in the reading rather than the whole passage are probably incorrect answers.

If you are not sure which answer is best, review the passage a second time by **skimming** — reading the passage quickly to get a sense of what the author is focusing on.

Let's practice a *main idea question*. Read the informational passage on the next page. Then answer the question that follows.

The temperature of the water in the Antarctic and Arctic Oceans is below freezing most of the year. The water surface is likely to be covered with ice for ten months of the year. Fish, such as the dragonfish, swim in the very cold waters below the ice. Salt in the water helps to keep this water from freezing. A special sugar-like substance in the blood of the fish, called glycopeptide, helps to keep ice from forming inside the fish. Like antifreeze in a car's radiator, it keeps the water from turning into ice. Glycopeptide keeps the blood of these fish from freezing. This natural antifreeze sticks to any tiny ice crystals that form in the blood. The glycopeptide prevents the crystals from growing large enough to be damaging.

1. **What is the main idea of this passage?**

   A Water in the Arctic and Antarctic Oceans is below freezing for most of the year.

   B A sugar-like substance in the blood of some fish allows them to swim in freezing-cold saltwater.

   C Glycopeptide is the name of a substance found in the blood of the dragonfish.

   D Antifreeze keeps the water in a car radiator from turning to ice.

The correct answer to this question is "**B**." The article explains that some fish can swim in the salt water of the Arctic and Antarctic, even though it is below freezing temperatures. A sugar-like substance prevents their blood from freezing. The other choices, although *correct* statements, are *not* the right answer. They focus on details in the article, not on the article's main message.

FINDING THE THEME OF A STORY

You already know that a story may have one or more themes. A ***theme*** is like the main idea of a reading. It is the most important message that the story tells. Details in the story develop the message. Themes provide lessons about life and human nature. For example, in *The Golden Touch,* we learn that it is wrong to be greedy. The story explains this theme by telling what happened to King Midas.

Some questions will ask about the theme of a story. Sometimes the theme is stated directly in the story. At other times, you need to figure out the theme. To find the theme, ask yourself the question in the box. Your answer will lead you to the theme of the story.

> What lesson about life did I learn from reading this story?

Let's practice answering a *theme question* about a story. First, read the passage below. Then complete the box and answer the multiple-choice question that follows.

"Why do you walk sideways?" said a mother crab to her young son. "You should walk straight with your toes turned out." Not sure what to do, the son said, "Show me how to walk, mother." The young crab was very respectful, and always did as his mother said. So the mother crab tried to walk forward. After several failed attempts, she could only walk sideways like her son. And every time she turned her toes out, she tripped and fell on the sand. The mother crab thought to herself that today she had learned an important lesson from her son.

Before you answer the multiple-choice question that follows this story, think about and write your answer to this question first:

BEING AN ACTIVE READER

What lesson about life did I learn from reading this story?

_____

_____

_____

_____

_____

2. **What lesson can we learn from this story?**
    A You should never expect thanks from those you help.
    B You are judged by the company you keep.
    C Don't tell others how to act unless you can do it yourself.
    D Take what you can get when you can get it.

Practice Exercises

Directions: Read the story. Then answer the question that follows.

COME RAIN OR SHINE
by Geary Smith

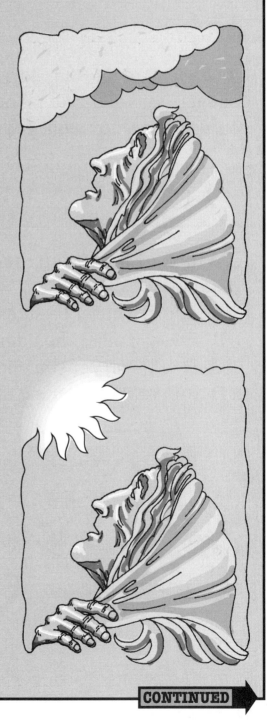

Years ago, there lived an old woman with two sons. The old woman was very poor. She depended on her sons to take care of her with what they earned in their businesses.

The woman's older son sold fans. Her younger son sold umbrellas. Every day, she worried about their businesses, praying they would make a lot of money.

Every morning at sunrise, the woman looked up to the sky. When it was cloudy and dark, she'd say, "If the sun doesn't shine today, nobody will want to buy my son's fans, and he won't make any money."

When the sun was shining, she'd say, "I'm sure nobody will want to buy umbrellas from my son today, and he won't make any money."

No matter how the sky looked, sunny or cloudy, the woman worried.

CONTINUED ▶

One evening, while fretting about the sort of weather the next day might bring, she came upon a close friend who knew of her situation.

"Do you think it will be sunny or cloudy tomorrow?" the old woman asked her friend.

"My dear, you should never worry what tomorrow will bring," replied the woman's friend. "You have two hard-working sons. If the sun is shining, your older son will make money. If it rains, your younger son will make money. No matter what tomorrow brings, you will be well provided for."

The woman thought about what her friend told her, and she was happy and content for the rest of her days.

1. **Which of these sentences gives us the main message of the story?**
   A You can never be sure about the weather.
   B Every mother should have two hard-working sons.
   C Don't worry if you don't really have a problem.
   D It is very frightening to grow old.

CHAPTER 10

ANSWERING OPEN-ENDED QUESTIONS ABOUT A READING

Sometimes you may be asked to write an answer to a question about a reading. This type of question is often called an **open-response question.** Unlike a multiple-choice question, this type of question requires you to do more than select the best choice from three or four possible answers. Instead, you must write out the answer in one or more sentences of your own. There are two types of open-ended questions:

SHORT-RESPONSE QUESTIONS

EXTENDED-RESPONSE QUESTIONS

SHORT-RESPONSE QUESTIONS

Short-response questions, also known as **short-answer questions,** require an answer from one or two words to several sentences. They usually focus on the details of a reading. Here are two typical short-response questions, based on *The Golden Touch* on page 18.

 Name the main characters of *The Golden Touch.*

 What was the "golden touch" in the story?

SOME KEY RULES FOR WRITING SENTENCES

★ Each sentence should express a complete thought.

★ Each sentence should have a subject and a predicate.

★ Make sure the subject and verb agree (singular / plural).

★ Begin each sentence with a capital letter.

★ Use the correct end punctuation (**.** / **?** / **!**) to finish each sentence.

EXTENDED-RESPONSE QUESTIONS

Extended-response questions ask for an answer of one or more paragraphs. This means you have to write a more thoughtful, detailed answer. There are three steps to answering extended-response questions:

★ **Step 1: Analyze the Question.** Carefully read the question and any specific directions it contains.

★ **Step 2: Plan and Write Your Answer.** Next think about your answer. Review the passage for ideas and details that help you to answer the question. Jot down notes with details from the reading. Then turn your notes into a graphic organizer or outline for answering the question. Include an introduction stating what you are writing about. Write your answer by turning each point of your graphic organizer or plan into a complete sentence.

★ **Step 3: Review and Revise Your Answer.** Now read over your work to make sure it makes sense and answers the question completely. Cross out information that does not belong, and add anything you left out.

QUESTIONS ABOUT OVERALL MEANING

Some extended-response questions test your general understanding of the story or reading passage in the story or what the reading was mostly about.

QUESTIONS THAT ASK YOU TO RETELL A STORY

Some questions ask you to **retell** the story. Write as much of the story as you can remember, *using your own words*. You should include important story details, like the setting, the names of the main characters, and the key events in the plot.

QUESTIONS THAT ASK YOU TO SUMMARIZE A STORY

Other extended-response questions ask you to **summarize** a passage. When you write a summary, you state the main ideas without the details. Summarizing tells someone else about the reading in a shortened form.

HINTS FOR ANSWERING A SUMMARIZING QUESTION

*When you **summarize** a **story** remember to:*

★ State the problem or challenge faced by the characters.

★ Give key events in the plot and show how the problem is resolved.

★ State any theme or lesson that can be learned from the story.

---

*When you **summarize** an **informational reading** remember to:*

★ Give the main idea of the reading.

★ Explain how the author supports the main idea, but don't give details.

Hint

Let's look at a typical extended-response question examining your overall understanding of a passage.

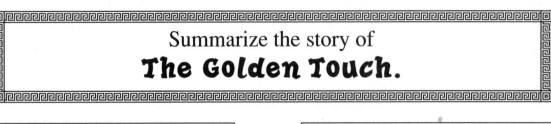

Summarize the story of
The Golden Touch.

> These sentences give the most important events in the plot.

> This sentence states the challenge faced by the main character.

In *The Golden Touch,* King Midas is granted one wish by the god Dionysus. Midas asks that everything he touches turns to gold. At first, Midas is happy when his wish is granted. His delight does not last when he finds that even his food and drink turn to gold when he touches them. Dionysus later helps Midas by taking away his ability to turn everything into gold. The story shows that we do not always find happiness when we want something out of greed.

> Here we learn about the story's theme or lesson.

> Here we learn how the problem is resolved.

QUESTIONS THAT FOCUS ON READING DETAILS

Both short-response and extended-response questions may focus on your understanding of specific details in a reading passage. Most questions will ask you about the **what, why,** and **how** of the passage. These question words provide the key to what you will have to do.

You already studied these question words in **Chapter 2.** Let's look at each of these question words again to see how they might appear in an open-response question.

WHAT QUESTIONS

The question word *what* asks you to identify, explain, or describe specific things in a reading passage.

Here are examples of how you might see a *what question:*

★ *What* did King Midas do to help the friend of Dionysus?

★ *What* did Midas ask for when he was granted a wish?

★ *What* was the main lesson of the story?

To answer a *what question,* first think about what the question asks for. Do you have to identify something, explain it, or describe it? Look over the reading to get ideas for answering the question. Next, jot down your ideas using some type of note form or graphic organizer.

Now you are ready to answer the question. Begin with a **topic sentence** that tells your reader what you are trying to *identify, explain,* or *describe.* The simplest way to form the topic sentence is to echo the question. **Echoing the question** means you repeat part of the question as a statement. Then use details from the reading as supporting details for the rest of your answer.

Let's look at a model answer to the last question above.

What was the main lesson of the story?
Explain your answer using details from the story.

This topic sentence echoes the question and gives the story's main lesson.

The main lesson of the story is that what we wish for often is not what is best for us. King Midas wanted the golden touch. He soon realized that this wish was really a curse. Midas could have all the gold he wanted, but he could not enjoy eating a piece of bread or drinking a glass of water. In the end, Midas realized that the simple pleasures in life, like eating and drinking, are more important than having gold. What he had thought he wanted was not really the best thing for him.

This sentence uses details and examples directly from the story to support the topic sentence.

The final sentence provides a strong conclusion to the paragraph by summing up the main idea.

CHECKING YOUR UNDERSTANDING

Now you try it.

What did King Midas do to earn a wish from Dionysus? Explain your answer using details from the story.

HOW QUESTIONS

How means "in what way." *How questions* look at what things are like in a reading, the way something happens in a reading, or the way something changes. Here are some examples of *how questions:*

> ★ *Explain how* Midas was able to turn things into gold.
>
> ★ *Tell how* the golden touch turned out to be a curse.
>
> ★ *Tell how* King Midas changed after he received the golden touch.

To answer a *how question,* first think about what the question asks for. Look over the reading to get ideas to help you answer the question. Quickly jot down your ideas using notes or a graphic organizer. For example, if the question asks you *how* something changed, you might list the steps or events in the passage that show how that thing or person has changed over the course of the reading.

Now you are ready to write your answer. Begin with a topic sentence that tells the reader what you are explaining. Again, you might want to echo part of the question. Use material from the reading as supporting details in your answer.

Let's look at a model answer to the third question above to see how you can apply what you have learned.

> *Tell how* King Midas changed
> after he received the golden touch.
> Explain your answer using details from the story.

This topic sentence echoes the question.

This part of the paragraph tells what Midas was like before he received the golden touch.

King Midas changed after he received the golden touch. Before he had the golden touch, all he thought about was having a good time and getting rich. When he was first received the golden touch, he was happy. Everything he touched turned to gold. He would be the richest man in the world. Midas soon found that anything he tried to eat or drink also turned to gold. He quickly became hungry and thirsty. Midas went to Dionysus and begged him to take away the golden touch. Midas learned that the simple pleasures in life are more important than having gold.

This part of the paragraph shows us how Midas changed after he received the golden touch.

CHECKING YOUR UNDERSTANDING

Now you try it.

Explain how the golden touch of King Midas turned out to be a curse. Explain your answer using details from the story.

_____

_____

_____

_____

_____

WHY QUESTIONS

Why questions look at causes and effects. A *why question* may ask you to give one or more reasons *why* something happened. A *why question* might also ask you for the effects of an event. Here are some typical examples of the ways a *why question* might appear:

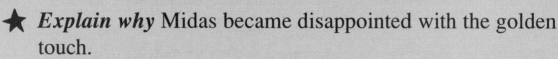

★ *Why* did Dionysus grant King Midas one wish?

★ *Explain why* Midas became disappointed with the golden touch.

When you answer a *why question,* first think about whether the question asks for *causes* or *effects.*

★ If the question asks about causes, think about the forces or events that caused the action or event to take place.

★ If the question asks why a character did something, think about the reasons that led the character to act that way.

★ If the question asks about effects, think about what happened because of that action or event.

Next, you should look over the reading to get ideas for your answer. Look for causes and effects. Jot down your ideas using notes or a graphic organizer. Often a topic or sequence map is useful for showing cause and effect.

Now you are ready to write your answer. Begin with a topic sentence that echoes the question. Be sure that your topic sentence makes clear what you are about to tell the reader. Then use details from the reading passage to provide supporting details.

Let's look at a model answer to the second question on this page.

Explain why Midas became disappointed
with the golden touch.
Explain your answer using details from the story.

> This topic sentence echoes the question and states the main idea of the paragraph.

> This part of the paragraph uses story details to explain why Midas became disappointed.

King Midas became disappointed with the golden touch for one reason. The golden touch gave Midas the power to turn everything he touched to gold. Midas soon discovered that he could not enjoy the simple pleasures of life, like eating and drinking. Whenever he tried to eat or drink something, it immediately turned to gold. Because Midas quickly grew hungry and thirsty, he became disappointed with the golden touch. He realized the golden touch was really a curse, not a gift.

> These last two sentences concludes the paragraph by summing up why Midas was disappointed.

CHECKING YOUR UNDERSTANDING

Now you try it.

What effects did the golden touch have on King Midas?
Explain your answer using details from the story.

_____

_____

_____

CHAPTER 11

TESTING YOUR UNDERSTANDING

This chapter will require you to read two passages. The first is an informational reading. The second is a story. Each passage is followed by a group of multiple-choice and extended-response questions. These questions test your understanding of different types of multiple-choice questions you have learned about in the last six chapters.

You should take about **45 minutes** to complete the questions about each passage. This will help you get an idea of how long it will take to complete multiple-choice questions when you take a real test.

Directions. First, you are going to read a passage with the title "The Celebrated Frogs with Missing Legs." Then you will answer several multiple-choice questions about what you have read. You may look back at the passage as often as you like. Now begin.

The Celebrated Frogs With Missing Legs

adapted from Susan Hayes

In the summer of 1999, eight students and their teacher were hiking in the woods near Henderson, Minnesota, as part of their study of the environment. But they soon came upon some frogs with twisted legs. "At first, we thought the frogs had broken their legs," said one of the students. "Then we found three or four frogs that were missing a leg."

The students headed to a nearby pond to search for more frogs. "The closer we got to the pond, the more problems we found," said another student. By the end of the day, they caught 22 frogs. Half of them had serious deformities.

The case of the frogs with missing legs alarmed scientists across the country. Scientists wanted to know what had happened to the frogs, and if what affected them could affect us.

The students wrote down their findings and returned to school with three of the frogs with missing legs. Because they found so many frogs with deformities, they thought the cause might be from chemicals sprayed on the surrounding farmland. They called the farmer who lived nearby to find out what pesticides he used. They placed queries on the Internet, asking if anyone else had seen similar frogs. Their teacher called the Minnesota Pollution Control Agency (*known as the M.P.C.A.*), a state agency that protects the environment.

CONTINUED

The M.P.C.A. decided to investigate. What happens to frogs is important because frogs act as early warning signs of a problem with the environment. Because their skin is so thin, they are easily hurt by poisons in both the air and water.

The M.P.C.A. immediately sent a researcher to the pond. The students were not content just to let the scientists take over. M.P.C.A. researchers assigned the students to find a control site — a place where there weren't any frogs with missing limbs.

"We must have checked out more than a dozen ponds," says Cindy. "We'd catch 100 normal frogs, but then we'd go back and find frogs with deformities."

News of the students' discovery spread. Reports started coming in from other states and foreign countries that similar outbreaks had been spotted. The frog mystery became an ongoing science project at the school. The kids — there were now 12 of them — were called the "Frog Group." Once a week, they headed for the pond, tested the water, and sent their results to the M.P.C.A.

Members of the group have testified before the state legislature to obtain funding for an educational program on frogs. They've created their own special frog web site. They even created an exhibit about the project at the Minnesota Zoo. They have appeared on television shows, including the Discovery Channel.

CONTINUED →

Today, scientists don't appear any closer to an explanation. The M.P.C.A. believes some kind of pollution in the water may be causing the deformities. Other scientists insist that the cause may be a natural one, such as parasites.*

"We're not sure what's causing it," says a Frog Group member. "Maybe it's a combination of things. Our goal is to inform people as to what is going on." Whoever finally solves the mystery, the students can take credit for finding it.

---

*__parasite__ – an animal or plant that lives off another animal or plant for its nutrients.

Each question is identified by its type. If you get a particular question wrong, re-read the section that tells you how to answer this type of question.

1. **What is this article mostly about?**
   A How young children learn
   B The importance of frogs in our lives
   C The mystery of the frogs with deformities
   D The important role played by the M.P.C.A.

   Opening Impressions

2. **In the article, students "placed queries on the Internet, asking if anyone else had seen similar frogs." What are *queries*?**
   A questions   C quotes
   B clever remarks   D reports

   Vocabulary

3. **Who first discovered that some frogs were missing legs?**
   A a school principal   C the M.P.C.A
   B some students   D scientists

   Specific Detail

4. **When did the events in this article first begin?**
   A summer   C winter
   B fall   D spring

   Specific Detail

5. **Where did the students find most of the frogs with deformities?**
   A in orchards on a farm   C in the woods
   B in a city sewer system   D in mobile homes

   Specific Detail

6. **What is the main job of the M.P.C.A.?**
   A It helps students learn about their surroundings.
   B It brings criminals to trials.
   C It is responsible for protecting the environment.
   D It provides scientific information over
      the Internet.

   Specific Detail

7. **Which sentence from the article expresses an opinion?**
   A The frogs with deformities alarmed scientists.
   B The students documented their findings and returned to school.
   C The students helped the M.P.C.A. collect frogs that were
      missing legs.
   D Some kind of pollution in the water may be
      causing the deformities.

   Fact/Opinion

8. **Which of these events in the article occurred first?**
   A The students asked the farmer about the pesticides he used.
   B Eight students were hiking in the woods in order to study
      their surroundings.
   C The students appeared on television.
   D The students created an exhibit at the
      Minnesota Zoo.

   Sequence

9. **Which word best describes the students in this story?**

   A curious   **C** affectionate

   B immature   **D** uncaring

> Pulling-It-Together

10. **What event would resolve the "mystery" in the article?**

   A if the school allowed students to take a class studying their surroundings

   B if scientists found the reason why the frogs were missing legs

   C if students became scientists when they grew up

   D if the state legislature voted that the mystery was solved

> Prediction

EXTENDED-RESPONSE QUESTION

11. **Why were the students so interested in the mystery of the frogs? Use details from the reading passage to support your answer.**

_____

_____

_____

_____

_____

_____

_____

_____

STOP

THE RECITAL
by Kathleen Benner Duble

"Hannah?" Mama said, bending down to her. "Are you all right?"

Hannah nodded yes. But it wasn't true. Since this morning her stomach had been doing flips like that day on the water slide when it kept going faster and faster and wouldn't slow down. When she had reached the bottom, she threw up on the sidewalk in front of millions of people. Thinking of this made Hannah feel even sicker.

"You're not nervous, are you?" Mama said. Hannah shook her head no.

"Why would she be scared?" Mary piped up. "She only has to play 'Twinkle, Twinkle, Little Star.' It's so easy I never practice it anymore. Besides, I'll be playing it with her. I'm the one who should be scared."

At the mention of "Twinkle," Hannah felt her stomach turn again. She thought of the piano waiting at Mrs. Johnson's studio, and her mouth suddenly felt dry and sticky. Mary picked up her violin and began to play a piece of music. It sounded beautiful to Hannah. It was something that would be too hard for her to play.

"I should be very nervous," Mary said, "I have to play three pieces tonight. But I'm not scared."

Hannah knew Mary was not scared. Mary was never scared. Hannah wished she were more like Mary. Hannah stared at her own white blouse, dark skirt, white tights, and black shoes. She felt like a zebra.

CONTINUED ▶

Papa came into the room and scooped up Mary. "So, it's the big night, is it? I can't wait to hear my little musicians play." He grinned at Hannah. Hannah forced herself to smile back.

Papa hugged her against him, still holding Mary. "To the car," he said, "and on to Mrs. Johnson's studio."

Backstage, Hannah's hands were cold and damp as she felt on edge. All around, students were tuning their instruments — accordions, trumpets, and clarinets. Hannah peeked through the closed curtains at the stage. It looked huge. The piano looked as if it could open its lid and eat her.

"Places, everyone!" called Mrs. Johnson. Mary danced into line behind Hannah and the other younger children.

"Aren't you supposed to be back here with us, Mary?" an older girl whispered.

"I have to play with my sister first," Mary whispered back. "Then I'll be back here." Mary put her hand in Hannah's hand and squeezed it tight. "It'll be all right," she said softly. Weakly, Hannah squeezed back.

The curtain opened. The recital began. One child played, then another. Soon, she heard Mrs. Johnson announce her name and Mary's name. Slowly Hannah walked on to the stage with Mary behind her. Hannah's legs felt weak. The lights were bright.

CONTINUED ▶

Quickly, Hannah walked to the piano. Mary stood by her, and they bowed. There was clapping, and once again, Hannah felt an awful taste in her mouth. When the clapping stopped, Hannah slid onto the piano bench. Mary put her violin to her chin and smiled at Hannah.

Mary nodded, and Hannah began to play. She thought about playing and nothing else. Suddenly, Hannah heard something odd. Mary was not playing "Twinkle." Hannah didn't know what Mary was playing. Hannah couldn't believe it. Her sister, Mary, was making a mess out of a simple song like "Twinkle."

Hannah glanced over at Mary. Her face was white, and her hands were trembling on the violin. Then Hannah realized what had happened. Mary had forgotten the notes, and now she was scared.

"I should have practiced," Mary thought, almost crying. Hannah began whispering the notes to the song to Mary — *A, A, E, E, F-sharp* .... Slowly, Mary hit the notes in time with Hannah's playing. When they finished, they finished together.

The clapping was loud in Hannah's ears. When they bowed, Hannah took Mary's hand and squeezed. Mary's hand was damp and cold, but Hannah's hand was dry and warm. Backstage, Mary didn't say a word, but ran off to be with her friends.

"Were you nervous?" Hannah heard someone ask Mary. "Who, me?" said Mary. "I'm never scared."

Just then, Mary turned and caught Hannah's eye. Mary smiled, and Hannah smiled back. Hannah would never tell. Mary was her sister. Besides, deep inside Hannah, there was a place that felt comforted knowing that Mary, too, could be scared.

1. **What is the story mostly about?**
   A learning how to practice a musical instrument
   B Hannah and Mary's relationship with their parents
   C playing a piano
   D how two sisters act during a music recital

   `Opening Impressions`

2. **In this story, Hannah and her sister Mary are at a recital. What does *recital* mean?**
   A the tuning of musical instruments
   B a musical performance
   C practicing a musical instrument
   D a meeting with other children

   `Vocabulary`

3. **In the story, Hannah's hands were cold and damp as she felt "on edge." What does *on edge* mean?**
   A nervous   C neighborly
   B never-ending   D sickly

   `Vocabulary`

4. **Who proved to be the most nervous character in the story?**
   A Mama   C Hannah
   B Mrs. Johnson   D Mary

   `Specific Detail`

5. **What happened to Hannah on the day she went for a ride on the water slide?**
   A She enjoyed herself tremendously.
   B She fell down and sprained her ankle.
   C She became ill and threw up.
   D She played the piano for some strangers.

   `Specific Detail`

6. **What musical instrument did Mary play?**
   A the piano   C a trumpet
   B a violin   D an accordion

   `Specific Detail`

7. **In the story, what do *A, A, E, E, F-sharp* stand for?**
   A the notes to a song in the story
   B the words to *Twinkle, Twinkle, Little Star*
   C a secret code used by Mary and Hannah
   D the sound made by dance steps

   Specific Detail

8. **What happened when Mary forgot the notes to "Twinkle"?**
   A Hannah took Mary's hand and squeezed it.
   B Hannah told everyone Mary forgot how to play the song.
   C Hannah began whispering the notes to the song to Mary.
   D Mary admitted her nervousness when she
      played the song.

   Sequence

9. **What led Hannah to become nervous in the story?**
   A She was afraid of making her mother angry.
   B She feared playing at the recital.
   C She was worried she would offend Mary.
   D She thought her father would be upset
      with her.

   Explanation

10. **In what way was Hannah similar to her sister?**
    A They were both expert piano players.
    B Neither sister was nervous.
    C Both sisters had spent a great deal of
       time practicing.
    D Both sisters were nervous at the recital.

    Compare-and-Contrast

11. **The author writes that the "piano looked as if it could open its lid and eat her" to show that Hannah**
    A was afraid
    B hated music
    C was hungry
    D would play piano

    Pulling-It-Together

12. The next time Mary participates in a recital at Mrs. Johnson's studio, she will most likely

   A practice before her performance

   B eat a large meal before leaving home

   C go to bed early the night before

   D wear different clothing than her sister does

Prediction

EXTENDED-RESPONSE QUESTION

13. What is the main lesson of the story? Use details from the story to support your answer.

_____

_____

_____

_____

_____

_____

_____

_____

_____

_____

_____

STOP

UNIT 2: WRITING

The second part of this book will help you to improve your writing skills. In this unit, you will learn a variety of writing styles and practice writing in response to different directions. Writing is the reverse of reading. You use words to record your thoughts and ideas. Someone who reads your words should be able to understand your ideas.

CHAPTER 12

TOOLS FOR WRITING

This chapter will introduce you to the tools you need to write well. Before we look at what it takes to be a good writer, let's see what *you* think is needed to write well.

THINK ABOUT IT

What do you think makes someone a good writer?

When you wrote your answer, you probably followed two steps:

 First, you had to think about what you wanted to say.

★ Second, you had to express your thoughts in words.

Good writers write clearly so that readers understand the thoughts they are expressing. A reader should be able to picture in his or her mind the same thoughts the writer was trying to express.

120

*The writer is able to write down thoughts
in a way that the reader can picture the same thoughts.*

THE BASIC TOOLS OF WRITING

There are **three basic tools** for writing: *words, sentences,* and *paragraphs.*

WORDS

PARTS OF SPEECH

There are many kinds of words. We sometimes label a word by its **part of speech.** This has to do with the role the word plays in a sentence.

★ **Nouns.** A noun is a word that names a person, place, or thing. Examples of nouns are: *man, house, town,* and *apple.*

★ **Pronouns.** A pronoun is a word that takes the place of a noun used earlier in the writing. Examples of pronouns are: *I, we, you, he, she, her, him, they,* and *it.*

★ **Verbs.** Verbs tell what a person or thing is doing or feeling or what is being done to it. Verbs are action words, because they describe some kind of action. Examples of verbs are: *jump, walk, run, dance, eat, think, feel, have* and *is.*

★ **Adjectives.** An adjective describes a noun. Adjectives add color and mood to a sentence. Examples of adjectives are: *red, rich, soft, beautiful, sad,* and *kind.*

★ **Adverbs.** Adverbs tell about verbs, adjectives, or even other adverbs. They are used by writers to tell *where, when,* and *how* an action happens. Examples of adverbs are: *often, quickly, never, always, very,* and *slowly.*

★ **Prepositions.** A preposition tells about the position of a noun or pronoun. It links the noun or pronoun to the rest of the sentence. Examples of prepositions are: *with, over, above, below* and *of.*

CHECKING YOUR UNDERSTANDING

Identify the part of speech of the following words:

quickly _____   slept _____

lemon _____   him _____

is _____   to _____

crunchy _____   green _____

SENTENCES

WHAT IS A SENTENCE?

A sentence is a group of words that expresses a complete thought. The first word in a sentence is always capitalized. Every sentence must end with a *period, question mark,* or *exclamation point*. Each sentence always has a subject and a predicate.

★ The **subject** is *who* or *what* the sentence is about. The subject is a noun or pronoun.

★ The **predicate** is what the subject *does* or *what happens to the subject* in the sentence. It provides the action of the sentence. The predicate uses a verb.

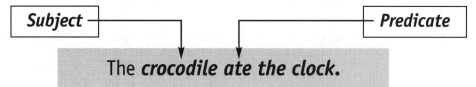

Subject ┐   ┌ Predicate

The **crocodile ate the clock.**

Together, the subject and predicate of a sentence should express a complete thought. If you read a sentence by itself, it should make sense to you. Do not be fooled by a group of words that look like a sentence. If they do not express a complete thought, they do not make up a sentence. An incomplete sentence is sometimes called a sentence *fragment*.

CHECKING YOUR UNDERSTANDING

Check (✔) the examples that are complete sentences.

❏ Before I went to school.   ❏ He ate fish yesterday.

❏ They watched television.   ❏ Because she was thirsty.

You should also avoid run-on sentences. A **run-on sentence** consists of several sentences joined together, usually by commas. It just runs on and on. You can correct a run-on sentence by breaking it up or adding words like **and** or **but**.

Run-on Sentence	It started raining, he went inside, he ate three tacos.
How to Fix it	When it started raining, he went inside and ate three tacos.

PARAGRAPHS

A **paragraph** is a group of sentences that deals with the same subject or theme. Each new paragraph is always **indented.** Often, a paragraph has a **topic sentence** that identifies the subject of the paragraph. The rest of the paragraph has details that tell about the subject identified by the topic sentence.

CHECKING YOUR UNDERSTANDING

Erica enjoys her job as an elementary school teacher. She loves watching her students' faces when they learn something for the first time. She also likes learning more about the different subjects she has to teach. Most of all, she feels that she is making a contribution to the world by helping the young people in her classroom to become responsible citizens.

★ Underline the topic sentence of this paragraph.

★ If you were writing this paragraph and wanted to add some more details about Erica, what other details might you write?

_____

_____

_____

There is no general rule about how long a paragraph should be. However, if your paragraph is very long, it can probably be broken down into two or more paragraphs. See if information in the paragraph can be divided up, based on different aspects of the topic.

CHAPTER 13

THE ELEMENTS OF GOOD WRITING: FOCUS AND SUPPORT

At the beginning of the last chapter, you thought about what it takes to be a good writer. A good writer has to be able to use the tools of writing — *words, sentences,* and *paragraphs* — with accuracy and skill. In particular, good writing has four important elements. The elements of good writing are:

1 FOCUS
2 SUPPORT
3 ORGANIZATION
4 WRITING CONVENTIONS

In this chapter we will look at the first two of these — *focus* and *support*. Later chapters will explore *organization* and *writing conventions*.

FOCUS

Focus means your writing stays on the topic you are writing about. You should identify the topic near the beginning of your writing. Tell your readers the purpose of your writing, so they will understand what they are about to read.

Everything you write about should stay focused on that topic. Think of your topic as an umbrella that covers your essay. You should have one or more main ideas you want to write about that topic. The details you add to your writing should support your main ideas. Avoid including information that does not relate to your topic.

CHECKING YOUR UNDERSTANDING

*Suppose you were writing about your classroom pet. Place a check mark (✔) next to all the sentences that would be **outside** the focus of your writing.*

❑ Our classroom pet is Mr. Whiskers, a white rabbit.

❑ This Thursday, we will be seeing a movie in class.

❑ Mr. Whiskers eats lettuce, carrots, and other vegetables.

❑ Mr. Whiskers lives in a cage at the back of our classroom.

❑ Each day we clean the cage and give Mr. Whiskers fresh water.

❑ Gerbils make good classroom pets, too.

When writing one or more paragraphs on a **test,** the focus will usually be provided by a writing prompt. A **prompt** is something that makes you think and respond. On a writing test, you respond to the prompt by writing.

A writing prompt can take many forms. It could be a short reading passage or a picture. It could also consist of simple directions on what to write about. Either way, the prompt will give you the topic you are to write about. On a writing test, be sure to keep your answer focused on the topic you chose in answering the prompt. Also, be sure to meet any requirement included in the writing prompt.

SUPPORT

Support refers to the details and examples you use to *explain, describe,* and *illustrate* your main ideas. You already know, for example, that an informational reading has supporting details that explain and describe the author's main idea. When you write, it is *your job* to provide the supporting details that explain your main idea. Always remember to add supporting details to your main idea.

★ **When You Explain Something.** If you are explaining something, give specific facts, details, and examples to support each part of your explanation. Put yourself in the reader's shoes. Think about what your reader needs to know to understand what you are explaining. Be sure to include those details.

CHECKING YOUR UNDERSTANDING

Explain why it is important that you go to school:

Reason: _____

_____

Reason: _____

_____

★ **When You Tell About Something.** If you are narrating a personal experience or retelling events from a story, describe each event in detail. Tell about the *who, what, when, where, how,* and *why* of each event. Be as specific as you can.

CHECKING YOUR UNDERSTANDING

Tell about your most favorite activity in the whole world:

What is it? _____

When do you do it? _____

Where do you do it? _____

How do you do it? _____

Why do you do it? _____

You already know that good readers create mental images as they read. When you write, you should try to do the same thing. You should try to give facts and details that will help your readers make mental images. Be as specific about what you are writing about as you can. Use all five senses — *sight, hearing, smell, touch,* and *taste* — to describe places, events, people, and things in detail. Use specific language to help your reader to see what you can see.

CHAPTER 14

THE ELEMENTS OF GOOD WRITING: ORGANIZATION

Organization, the third element of good writing, refers to how well you put your ideas together. Imagine someone who built a house with the roof at the bottom and the basement on top. The house would soon collapse!

In the same way, your writing has to be put together in a *logical* and *orderly* way. If your organization is not logical, your reader will not be able to follow what you are writing about.

Good writers usually organize what they write into three parts: the introduction, body and conclusion. The rest of this chapter looks at how each of these parts is organized.

THE INTRODUCTION

When we first meet someone new, we usually introduce ourselves. Similarly, when writing you should begin with an introduction. The introduction is where you tell your reader what your writing will be about. An introduction may be as short as a single sentence, or it could take up your entire first paragraph.

THE BODY OF YOUR WRITING

The body is the main part of your essay answer. Here is where you focus on giving details and examples to support the task or position taken in the introduction. Be as descriptive as possible. Use all five senses in describing things. Include plenty of details and examples to help your reader understand your ideas.

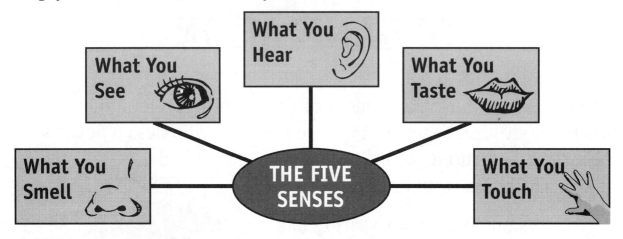

In the body of your essay, organize your ideas and details in some *logical order.* This makes it easy for the reader to follow your ideas. How you organize your writing will depend on what you are writing about. There are four ways good writers use to write in a logical order:

★ **Time Order.** If you are telling about an event or experience, the first paragraph should include an "umbrella" statement. This statement identifies the experience you will write about. Then tell about things in the order in which they happened. Start with the first event. Describe that event by telling about the *who, what, when, where, how,* and *why.* Then move on to the second event. Proceed in time order until you completely describe all the events that made up the experience.

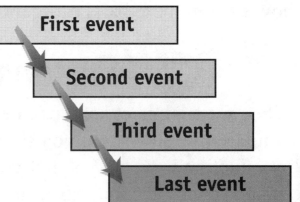

★ **Cause-and-Effect Order.** If you are explaining the causes and effects of an important event, one way is to begin by stating all of the causes. After you have stated all the causes of the event, then describe the event's effects. Another way to write about causes and effects is to identify each cause and its particular effects, one at a time.

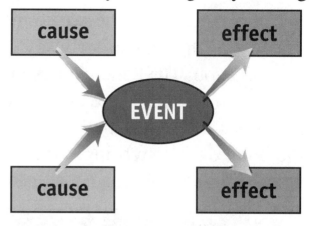

★ **Space Order.** If you are describing an object or scene in your writing, imagine the object or scene in your mind. Then pick some point and begin to describe it. Move left to right, or up and down as you continue your description. Be sure to continue in the same direction for the rest of the description.

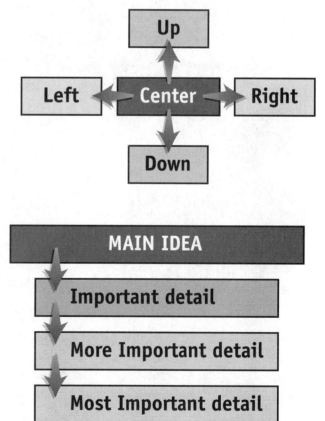

★ **Order of Importance.** If you have a main idea and a number of examples or supporting details, give the general or main idea first. Then provide the supporting details in order of their importance. Give the most important example or reason first. You can also start with the least important first, and move to the most important.

CONCLUSION

When we leave someone, we normally say good-bye. At the end of your essay, you should similarly say good-bye to your reader by writing a conclusion. The conclusion signals to the reader that the writing is coming to an end. There are many ways to conclude your writing. In your conclusion, you may want to briefly summarize the main ideas of the body of your writing. You may also want to state some general moral or lesson that can be learned from what you have written.

A NOTE ABOUT TRANSITION WORDS

An important part of organizing your writing is to use transition words. Transition words act as signposts for your readers. These words tell your readers that you are moving from one point to another. When readers see these signposts, they know they are moving in the right direction. Some useful transition words and phrases include:

★ When giving a list of points, use number words like first, second, and third. Each time the reader sees a new number, he or she will know that you have moved to a new idea or new point.

★ When telling about events, you can often use the day of the week or time of year as a transition. Other useful transitions include the next day, the following week, later that year, and next.

★ Other common transition words include: for example, therefore, also, in addition, another, and then.

THE USE OF PRONOUNS
TO HOLD YOUR ESSAY TOGETHER

Pronouns — such as *he, she, they,* and *their* — help "glue" your essay together by connecting sentences. If you use a noun, you can refer to it with a pronoun in later sentences. This helps to tie your writing together for the reader.

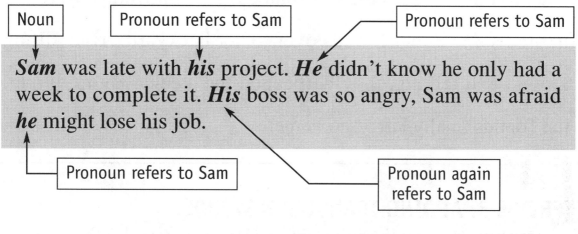

| Noun | Pronoun refers to Sam | | Pronoun refers to Sam |

Sam was late with **his** project. **He** didn't know he only had a week to complete it. **His** boss was so angry, Sam was afraid **he** might lose his job.

| Pronoun refers to Sam | | Pronoun again refers to Sam |

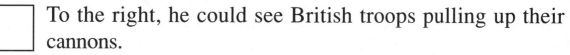

Practice Exercises

EXERCISE 1: ORGANIZING SENTENCES

Directions: *Number each of the following sentences in the order you would place them in a logically organized paragraph.*

[ ] To the right, he could see British troops pulling up their cannons.

[ ] Justin looked in amazement at the scene in front of him.

[ ] To the left he could see the red uniforms of the British troops.

[ ] In the center of the field, he could see hundreds of British cavalry.

[ ] Justin realized that he needed to send a message to General Washington at once.

EXERCISE 2: FINDING TRANSITION WORDS

Directions: *In the following paragraph,* (circle) *each word or phrase that is used as a transition:*

On Tuesday, Robin went to the bank. Later that evening, she bought some steaks at the supermarket. The following day, Robin invited some of her friends over to her backyard. After sitting around and talking, they barbecued the steaks. By midnight, her friends finally left to go home.

EXERCISE 3: ADDING TRANSITION WORDS

Directions: *Review the following sentences.* (Circle) *the transition words that you think best improve the logical flow.*

There are several reasons why violence on television is not good for young people. **First / Finally**, young people maybe influenced by what they see. Some children may start to think violence is safe. **Second / Therefore**, some children have nightmares. They become afraid that things they see on television will happen to them. **For example / Finally**, television violence is distracting. Many children who see a lot of television violence find it hard to concentrate on school work.

CHAPTER 15

THE ELEMENTS OF GOOD WRITING: WRITING CONVENTIONS

In addition to having good ideas, interesting details, and a logical organization, it is important to express yourself correctly when you write. Otherwise, readers will have a hard time understanding what you mean.

WHY WE HAVE WRITING CONVENTIONS

The fourth element of good writing is known as **writing conventions.** Conventions have been developed for standard spelling, grammar, capitalization, and punctuation. These conventions provide rules for how we should express ourselves. By following these standard rules for writing, we can understand each other more easily. In this chapter, you will learn some of the most important conventions for standard written English.

Writers most often make mistakes in the following areas:

Spelling	Capitalization	Punctuation	
	Subject-Verb Agreement	Pronouns	Tenses

Let's look at each of these six areas more closely to see what mistakes you should be aware of.

SPELLING

Hundreds of years ago there were no rules for spelling in English. People spelled each word in their own way. Today, we have rules for spelling words. Most words can be spelled in only one way.

Because the English language has been influenced by other languages, the same sound is not always spelled the same way. This makes it harder to know how to spell some words. When you misspell a word or learn a new word, you should look carefully at the word. Often there is a "hot spot" that makes the word difficult to spell. Focus on the "hot spot." Make a circle or box around it. Then write the word correctly several times from memory. Keep a list of words you have difficulty spelling. Practice spelling them correctly.

CHECKING YOUR UNDERSTANDING

Circle the "hot spot" in each of the following words.
The first has been done for you

Tuesday	weather	balloon	swimming
across	coming	pleasant	address
their	friend	afraid	separate
receive	there	February	Wednesday

CAPITALIZATION

You should always start each sentence with a capital letter. In addition, all proper nouns are capitalized. A **proper noun** is the name of a specific person, place, or thing. For example, *Samuel Adams, Boston,* and the *Declaration of Independence* are all proper nouns.

CHECKING YOUR UNDERSTANDING

Underline each letter of the following nouns that should be capitalized.

★ mr. smith   ★ bread   ★ strawberry jam

★ florida   ★ meat loaf   ★ disneyland

PUNCTUATION

Here are some of the main rules for the correct use of punctuation:

★ Use commas to separate items in a list, dates, quotations, and places in a sentence where you would pause. Also use commas to separate a city from its state or country.

> Lenny brought tomatoes, eggs, milk, and a loaf of bread to his hotel room in Paris, France. It was May 5, 1992.

★ Use periods at the end of abbreviations.

> Mr., Ms., Mrs., U.S.A.

★ Use apostrophes to show possession or contractions.

> Jack's boat   I'm = I am

★ Use quotation marks for direct speech.

> "I want to go home," she said loudly.

SENTENCE ENDINGS

You always end a sentence with a *period, question mark,* or *exclamation point.* The punctuation you use will depend on the type of sentence.

★ End each statement with a period.

> The hungry monkeys ate a bunch of bananas**.**

★ End each question with a question mark.

> What time is it**?**

★ End sentences that show strong feelings, such as surprise, laughter or some other strong emotion, with an exclamation point.

> You look absolutely ridiculous with that hat on your head**!**

CHECKING YOUR UNDERSTANDING

Add the final punctuation to each of these sentences.

★ The baker took the hot loaves of bread from the oven ☐

★ Where is the best place to buy a computer ☐

★ I have never been happier in all my life ☐

Insert the correct punctuation in the following paragraph:

It was late at night on October 13 ☐ 1995 ☐ Everything was quiet in the house ☐ Suddenly we heard a crash ☐ A large number of people rushed out of their homes to see what was going on ☐ ☐ Is anyone hurt ☐ ☐ our neighbor asked ☐ ☐ It looks like there was an earthquake ☐ ☐ my mother answered ☐

SUBJECT-VERB AGREEMENT

The subject and verb of a sentence should always "agree" with each other.

★ If the subject of a sentence is singular, you should use a verb in the singular form.

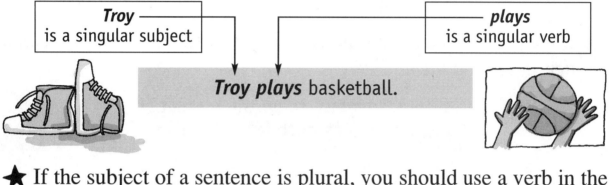

| ***Troy*** is a singular subject | | ***plays*** is a singular verb |

Troy plays basketball.

★ If the subject of a sentence is plural, you should use a verb in the plural form.

| ***Troy and Susan*** form a plural subject | | ***play*** is a plural verb |

Troy and Susan play basketball.

CHECKING YOUR UNDERSTANDING

See if you can choose the correct verb in each of the following:

1. They (***are eating / is eating***) lunch.

2. They (***have / has***) many pets in their home.

3. He (***wakes / wake***) up each morning at 7:00 o'clock.

4. Susan's grandmother (***live / lives***) in Dallas, Texas.

5. Joan (***walk / walks***) to school each morning.

PRONOUN FORMS

Pronouns take the place of nouns. Pronouns take different forms when they are used in different places in a sentence.

★ If the pronoun is the subject, use *I, you, he, she, it, we,* or *they.*

> ***He*** is going to karate class.

★ If the pronoun is not the subject of the sentence, use *me, you, him, her, it, us,* and *them.*

> Chinami gave ***them*** the present.
> Carson sent a birthday card to ***her***.

CHECKING YOUR UNDERSTANDING

Select the correct pronoun to complete the following sentences:

1. (***He / Him***) went to the zoo for a visit.

2. (***She / Her***) baked (***he / him***) a cake for his birthday.

3. (***They / Them***) like to go bowling on Saturday.

Some pronouns raise special problems. Here are three groups that often cause confusion:

★ **It's / Its**

It's is a contraction for two words — ***it*** and ***is***:

> ***It's*** time to go to bed.

Its without an apostrophe shows possession:

> The stray cat was missing ***its*** owner.

★ There / their / they're

There means a place:

He lives over ***there***.

Their shows possession:

Their car is waiting.

They're is a contraction for two words — *they are*:

They're going away.

★ Your / You're

Your shows possession:

Is this ***your*** boat?

You're means *you are*:

You're in a good mood today.

CHECKING YOUR UNDERSTANDING

Select the correct form of the word to complete the following sentences:

1. (***Its*** / ***It's***) time that we go home.
2. Is this (***your*** / ***you're***) hat and gloves?
3. (***There*** / ***Their*** / ***They're***) is where the monster lives.

VERB TENSES

Verbs take different forms, known as **tenses,** to tell us when an action takes place. Different tenses are used to express actions in the *present, past,* and *future.*

Past Tense	Present Tense	Future Tense
He liked her.	He likes her.	He will like her.
She was eating.	She is eating.	She will be eating.

When you write, be sure to keep your verbs in the right tense. If a story takes place in the past, keep all of the verbs you are using in the past tense. Change the tense of the verb only if the action moves to the present or future.

Last week, the grumpy sailor *ate* at the old inn. He *had* a meal of fish and *washed* it down with some wine. Then he *went* to sleep in the loft in the stables above the horses. Next week, he *will go* back to work with the new captain of the ship.

Notice how the first three sentences are all happening in the past. In the last sentence, the action switches to something that will take place in the future. As a result, the verb changes to the future tense.

COMBINING SENTENCES

It would be quite boring if every sentence was the same. Use different kinds of sentences to keep your writing interesting. You can combine sentences by using words such as *and* and *but*. You can also use special words like *since, because, who, while,* and *although* to combine sentences. Let's look at some examples:

Two Sentences

Peter likes to eat nuts.   Mary enjoys eating fruit.

One Sentence

Peter likes to eat nuts, *but* Mary enjoys eating fruit.

Two Sentences

Al went shopping in the store.
His sister Mary went to the library.

One Sentence

Al went shopping in the store, **while** his sister Mary
went to the library.

CHECKING YOUR UNDERSTANDING

*Combine the following pairs of sentences.
Use the word in parentheses to join them.*

(Who) Michael Jordan is a famous basketball player. He played
for the Chicago Bulls.

(But) I enjoy playing baseball. I do not like to play basketball.

CHECKING YOUR WRITING FOR ERRORS

A ship's lookout is constantly checking to be sure that nothing gets in the way of the ship's safety. When you write, you should play the role of a ship's lookout. You must always be on the lookout for writing errors. Keep reviewing what you are writing. This will help you catch writing errors that could distract and confuse your readers.

MULTIPLE-CHOICE QUESTIONS ON WRITING CONVENTIONS

Some classroom, district, and statewide tests use multiple-choice questions to see how well students follow the conventions of written English. These questions can take several forms.

 Some questions may ask you to choose which sentence is written correctly.

1. **Which of the following is written correctly?**
   A Americans declared their independence on July 4, 1776.
   B Americans declared their independence on july 4, 1776.
   C Americans declared their independence on July 4. 1776.
   D Americans declared their Independence on july 4. 1776.

 Some questions may ask you to distinguish a complete sentence from sentence fragments.

2. **Which of the following is a complete sentence?**
   A Because he wanted to sleep.
   B She ate a candy bar.
   C Not now.
   D At three o'clock.

3. **Which of these sentences in the paragrph below is NOT a complete sentence?**

   (1) Ben wanted to go home. (2) His mother wanted to stay. (3) At least until lunch. (4) Then she wanted to go, too.
   A Sentence 1
   B Sentence 2
   C Sentence 3
   D Sentence 4

★ Some questions may ask you the best way to combine two sentences. When combining sentences you can often remove repeated words or replace them with pronouns to make a better sentence. Also remember to use correct punctuation. Use a comma before ***and*** or ***but*** when using these words to combine whole sentences, but not for compound subjects or verbs.

4. *Deidre missed the bus. She arrived late to school.*

Which is the best way to combine these sentences without changing their meaning?

A Deidre missed the bus, and arrived late to school.
B Deidre missed the bus, but she arrived late to school.
C Because Deidre missed the bus, she arrived late to school.
D Deidre missed the bus, since she arrived late to school.

5. *He'll eat dinner. He'll go to sleep.*

Which is the best way to combine these sentences without changing their meaning?

A He'll eat dinner, and go to sleep.
B He'll eat dinner and go to sleep.
C He'll eat dinner, and he'll go to sleep.
D He'll eat dinner, or he'll go to sleep.

★ Some questions underline part of a sentence that may contain a mistake. You can either keep the sentence as it is or choose to replace the underlined part.

6. This time of year is my <u>favorite, all</u> the birds are singing.

A favorite. All   C favorite? All
B favorite, all   D favorite, All

7. They <u>was getting they're</u> things ready for the trip.

A was getting they're   C were getting their
B were getting they're   D was getting there

★ Questions on spelling may show you a sentence and ask you to identify which word is misspelled. You can also choose *"no error"* if each word in the sentence is spelled correctly.

8. On <u>Wednesday,</u> <u>there</u> was a <u>feirce</u> thunderstorm.
        A   **B**   **C**   **D** *NO ERROR*

9. He <u>received</u> the good <u>news</u> on <u>Teusday</u>.
    A   **B**   **C**   **D** *NO ERROR*

10. "<u>You're</u> <u>swimming</u> <u>to</u> close to the waterfall," he cried.
    A   **B** **C**   **D** *NO ERROR*

11. He <u>used</u> his <u>compass</u> to find his way out of the <u>canyon</u>.
    A   **B**   **C D** *NO ERROR*

★ You might be asked to answer an extended-response question on writing conventions. For example, you might be shown a sample student work. Then you would be asked to make any necessary corrections.

The following letter has several mistakes.

Dear Julie,

    Today was very important day? I bought my first pet. His name is piggles. He is a guinea pig. piggles eats lettuce hay and special pellets for guinea pigs. He live in a cage. Most of the day he sleeps, at night he runs around the cage. I plays with him every morning and after school.

               Your friend,
               Taylor

Using a sheet of your own paper, rewrite the letter without mistakes.

CHAPTER 16

RESPONDING TO A WRITING PROMPT

Often you will be given a task in the classroom or on a test in which you have to respond to a writing prompt. Your response should have *focus, support,* and *organization,* and follow *writing conventions.*

STEPS IN RESPONDING TO A WRITING PROMPT

There are four main steps in responding to such a writing prompt:

1 ANALYZE THE PROMPT

2 PLAN YOUR ANSWER

3 DRAFT YOUR ANSWER

4 EDIT AND REVISE

STEP 1: ANALYZE THE PROMPT

The prompt will have specific directions on what you have to write about. Sometimes you will have to answer a question. Other times, the prompt will identify a subject and tell you to write about it. A third type of prompt contains a short passage, picture or something else to stimulate your thinking. It then asks you to write about it. The prompt provides the focus for your writing.

Let's look at a sample writing prompt:

WRITING PROMPT

People do many different things for pleasure and relaxation on weekends. Some people like to go to the movies. Others enjoy a picnic.

Write an essay describing something fun and relaxing you enjoy doing on weekends. Tell about the activity and why it is fun for you.

To analyze this prompt, you should use the following steps:

★ First, you must determine the type of writing you are being asked to create. In the sample prompt, are you writing a description, telling about a personal experience, writing a creative story, or keeping a journal?

> *The first sentence of the second paragraph of the prompt tells you that you are being asked to write a descriptive essay.*

★ Examine the question words or commands in the prompt. Does the prompt ask you to **_tell about, explain how, explain why,_** or **_give reasons why_**? In the sample prompt, what are you asked to do?

> *In this sample prompt, you are asked to **describe** something you enjoy doing on weekends and to explain **why** it is fun for you.*

 Take a moment to think about the *task* in the prompt. Use any clues provided in the prompt to spur your thinking.

> *In this sample prompt, your task is to tell about a weekend activity. Think about a weekend activity **you** really enjoy.*

STEP 2: PLAN YOUR ANSWER

 The next step in the writing process is to **plan** your answer. For many students, this is the hardest part of responding to a prompt. You need to think of what you want to write about. One way to get ideas is to jot down notes on different items you might write about. Then look them over to see what best responds to the prompts directions.

After you select your main idea or have made a choice, start to fill in the details. It sometimes helps to create an **outline** or **topic map** to organize your thoughts about the task in the prompt. You already learned about topic maps in **Chapter 2.** Put your topic in the middle of the paper. Surround this topic with supporting facts and examples. Then number your points in the order you want to present them.

Another way is to create an outline in the form of a hamburger.

★ The **top bun** serves as your *introduction.*

★ The **patties of meat** form the *body of your answer.*

★ The **bottom bun** is your *conclusion.*

The top bun serves as the place where you identify the event you are describing, your main idea, or the position you are taking in response to the prompt.

The patties of meat make up the body of your essay. Here you list reasons, specific details, and examples to support the main idea you stated in the introduction.

The bottom bun serves as the place where you summarize your main ideas and remind the reader of your strongest points.

STEP 3: DRAFT YOUR ANSWER

In this third step, you turn your hamburger or other form of prewriting into a finished product. Turn each point of your plan into one or more complete sentences. Whatever form of prewriting you use, remember to organize your writing into the three parts of an essay — *introduction, body,* and *conclusion.* Make sure the body of your essay is logically organized and stays focused on the writing assignment.

STEP 4: REVISE AND EDIT YOUR ANSWER

The first person to read your response should be **YOU** — *not* the person grading your writing. Always read over your work before you hand it in. Read your draft silently to yourself. Pretend you are reading it for the first time. Make sure that you have included all your major ideas.

As you review what you have written, ask yourself some questions. If your answer is "no" to any of the following questions, your answer is not finished and needs further work:

★ Did you *follow directions* in the writing prompt?

★ Does your writing have a *focus*?

★ Have you *stayed on the topic*?

★ Do you have an *introduction, body,* and *conclusion*?

★ Does the body of your essay have a *logical organization*?

★ Have you *provided details, examples,* and *reasons* to support or explain your position or main idea?

★ *Could a person reading your paper for the first time understand what you mean?*

Revise your draft by rewriting sections that are poorly organized. Add ideas and details that you may have left out. Take out any information that does not relate to the question.

On a test, just cross out the sections you want to take out. Also edit your writing by checking for errors in writing conventions. Watch out for mistakes in spelling, grammar, punctuation, and usage.

You can use the proofreading marks shown below to help you edit.

COMMON PROOFREADING MARKS

> One of the *most* exciting and interesting things that *ever* happened to me
>
> was going to rome, *Italy,* with my mother. When I was nine *years old* my mother
>
> decided to take me *on a trip there* ~~along~~. My mother was ~~in charge~~ *the manager* of the dress
>
> department at a large *downtown* department store. Every Fall she would
>
> travel to Italy to ~~see~~ *preview* the newest fashions.

CHAPTER 17

WRITING ABOUT YOUR EXPERIENCES

In the last chapter, you learned how to respond to a writing prompt in general. The next several chapters deal with specific types of writing assignments. For example, you may be asked to write about your own personal experiences. This could be for a homework assignment, a class project, or a test.

You may feel somewhat uncomfortable writing about yourself and your own experiences. Remember, the purpose of writing about your experiences is *not* to tell others the details of your personal life. Your teacher is **less** concerned with your actual experiences than with your ability to write about them.

If you cannot recall all the details of an experience, you can make up some of them. When writing about an experience, you have to start at the beginning and describe each event in the order in which it happened. Taken together, these events should tell a common story or be related to a common theme.

When writing about your personal experiences, try to describe each event by telling about the:

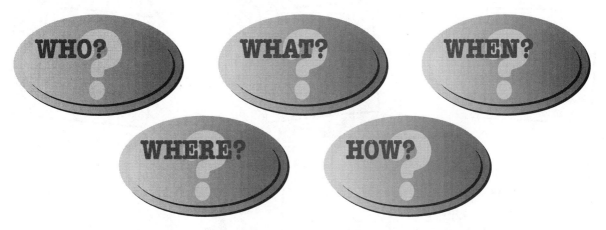

When you write a longer composition, you will usually be given a writing prompt. The prompt will tell you what to write about. For example, a writing prompt might ask you to write about something interesting that you did during your last summer vacation.

Often the hardest part of writing is to take that first step and start. As you know, the first step of the writing process is to analyze the prompt. To answer the sample prompt in the last paragraph, start by thinking hard about what you did last summer. Focus on one of the more interesting experiences you had. This experience may have involved something you did alone, with your family, or with friends.

The next step is prewriting. Jot down your ideas in an outline, sequence, or topic map. **Brainstorm** to think of as many details as you can. When you *brainstorm*, you jot down any ideas that come into your head, even if some do not seem very good. Afterwards, you review your notes to see which ideas are really good.

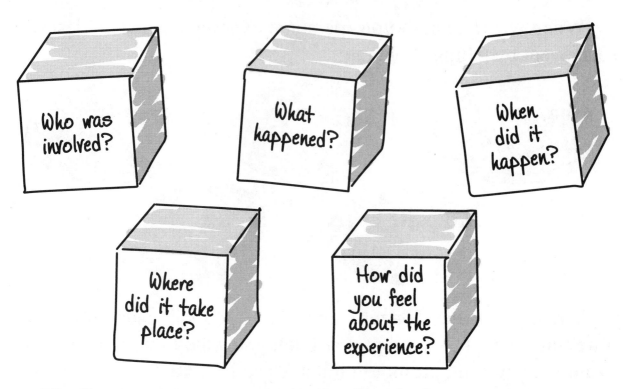

Finally, use your notes to write the first draft:

★ Keep your writing focused on the topic you are writing about — what you did last summer. Be sure that you have told the reader what you will be writing about.

★ Be sure to have a clear *introduction, body,* and a *conclusion.* Organize the body of your essay by time order, space order, or order of importance.

★ Include supporting details to make your answer interesting. Use all five senses to describe your experience. Remember, you know what you are writing about, but the person reading your essay has to have the details carefully described. The more details you provide, the easier it will be for the reader to "see" what you did last summer.

In the final step, edit and revise your work. Check your essay for errors in writing conventions. Be careful to avoid errors in grammar, usage, capitalization, punctuation, and spelling.

Here is a sample essay that one student wrote about his last summer vacation.

Notice how each paragraph is indented.

This paragraph introduces the topic of the essay.

Summer vacation is supposed to be a fun time. Many families go to the beach, visit museums, or stay home and watch television. Not my family! We took a trip to Disney World in Orlando, Florida. It was the most exciting and fun summer of my entire life.

This paragraph tells about one part of the vacation, the flight.

The flight was long and boring. The flight attendants served us food and drinks. Before long my sister and I fell asleep. When we woke, my mother was telling us we would be landing in Florida in twenty minutes.

Florida is such an interesting place. The weather was very hot. There were palm trees everywhere. Many of the buildings and hotels are painted a bright pink and turquoise color. The first afternoon we arrived in Florida we took it easy. We went swimming in the hotel's pool.

These next paragraphs give details about Orlando. The author tells what some of his senses experienced.

The next day we went to Disney World. It is a huge place. There are several different theme parks. In the Magic Kingdom we met Mickey Mouse and Donald Duck. My favorite ride was the Pirates of the Caribbean. I felt a lump in my stomach as we plunged down into the darkness. We enjoyed eating all kinds of delicious and different foods.

I have done lots of interesting things during past summer vacations. I was once on a swim team and won a medal for second place. But the best and most fun-filled vacation was the one my family took to Disney World.

The last paragraph ends with a conclusion.

Now you try it. Write a personal experience essay about what you did last summer. Like the model essay, try to provide details that will appeal to as many of the readers senses as you can.

Before you write your essay, plan what you are going to write by using the blank hamburger outline below. If you prefer, you can use some other prewriting technique.

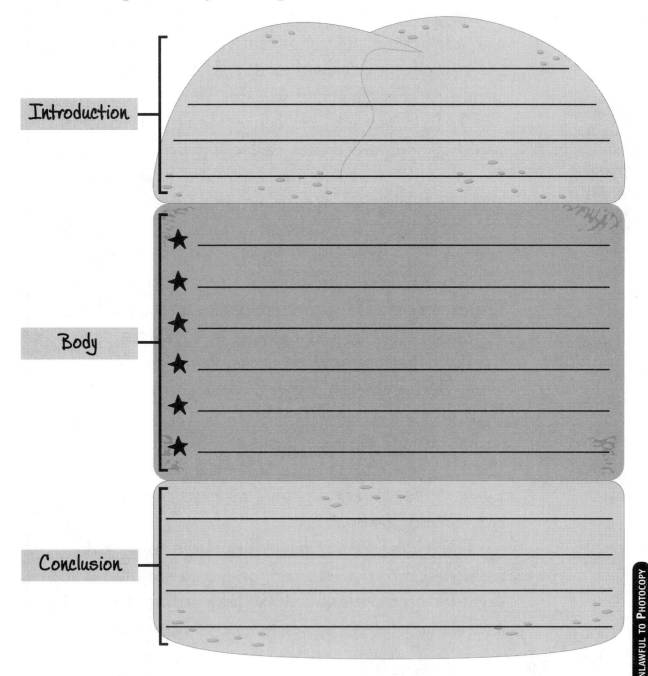

Introduction

Body

Conclusion

Now write your response below:

When you finish writing your essay, revise and edit your work. Remember, you are not finished until you have corrected any errors in what you wrote.

CHAPTER 18

WRITING A DESCRIPTIVE ESSAY

You may be asked to write a description of a person, place, or thing. Sometimes this kind of writing is known as an **expository** or **descriptive essay.** To *describe* means to "illustrate something in words or to tell about it." A description is almost like having an artist paint a picture. However, instead of using a brush, a writer "paints" with words.

SOME HELPFUL HINTS

An essay that provides a description should help the reader to see, feel, or hear what you are describing. Some helpful hints include:

 Make an outline or topic map in which you develop your main idea about the topic and decide what supporting details to include.

 Use all your senses to help you think of interesting details to include in your description. Use words that will help the reader to create a mental image of what you are describing.

★ Present your main ideas and supporting details in a logical order. Your organization should be clear. This can be done by using space order, time order, or order of importance.

★ Draft your essay with an introduction, body, and conclusion.

Suppose a writing prompt asked you to tell about an important place in the neighborhood where you live. Let's look at a model essay written in response to such a prompt:

A MODEL DESCRIPTIVE ESSAY

Notice how each paragraph is indented.

Notice how each paragraph begins with a topic sentence.

Notice how this introduction identifies the topic the author is going to write about.

Notice how the body of the essay provides details that explain the importance of the schoolhouse.

There are many buildings in my neighborhood. One of the most important buildings is the old schoolhouse on Maple Road.

The schoolhouse is one of the easiest buildings to spot. Built of red brick, it is the oldest building in our neighborhood. When the pioneers settled in our area, the schoolhouse was one of the first buildings they built. Today it is a museum.

The schoolhouse looks just as it did a hundred years ago. There are wooden desks, old books lined on shelves, and a globe on the teacher's desk from 1900. In the center of the schoolhouse is an old black iron stove.

It is not just the objects of this building that make the schoolhouse important. People often talk about what the building really means to our community. This schoolhouse shows the importance early settlers placed on education. Their love for learning is what makes this building important.

Notice how the essay concludes by tying the different parts of the essay together.

PRACTICE WRITING A DESCRIPTIVE ESSAY

Now you should practice writing a descriptive essay. Read the following prompt and then draft your essay.

> ### WRITING PROMPT
> We all enjoy visiting different places outside of our neighborhood. Think about a place outside of your neighborhood that you enjoyed visiting. Then write an essay that provides information about that place to someone who has never been there.

PREWRITING YOUR ESSAY

Now that you know what you must write about, spend a few moments thinking about what you're going to write. Then prewrite your essay using the hamburger outline or any other prewriting format you prefer:

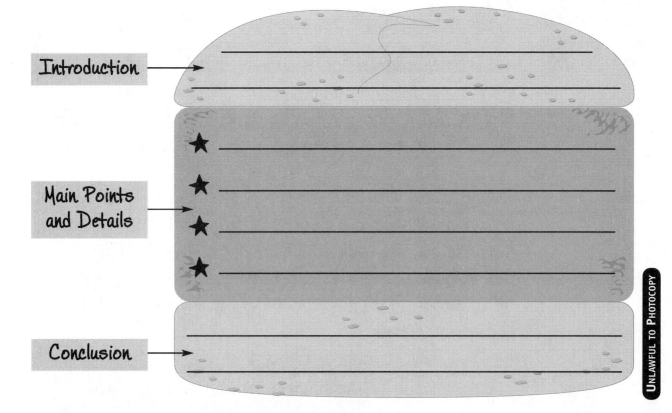

Introduction

Main Points and Details

Conclusion

Now write your essay below:

When you finish, revise and edit your essay. After you have checked your essay and are satisfied with it, you are finished.

CHAPTER 19

WRITING AN IMAGINARY STORY

Another type of writing assignment that you may have on a test, in class or at home is to write your own fictional or make-believe story. You have read many make-believe stories in school and at home. You also learned about the main parts of a story earlier in this book. In this chapter, you will learn how much fun it can be to write a make-believe story of your own.

HOW TO WRITE AN IMAGINARY STORY

You may be asked to write a story based on a writing prompt in a classroom assignment or on a test. If you are writing in response to a prompt, be sure to keep your story related to the topic of the prompt. Remember that your story should have three important parts:

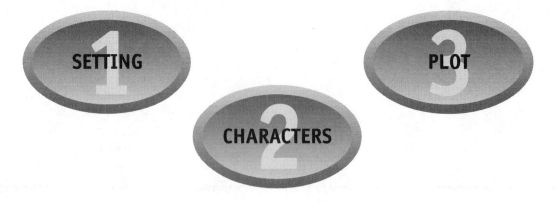

SETTING 1

CHARACTERS 2

PLOT 3

162

SOME HELPFUL HINTS TO GET STARTED

There are many approaches to writing a story. Whichever method you choose, here are some hints to help guide you:

 Start by focusing on the basic parts of your story — its *setting, characters,* and *plot.*

 Your story should have a clear focus. Begin with an interesting problem or challenge that the characters in your story must overcome.

★ Continue your story with a series of events that happen to your characters. As events unfold, they should make it easier or harder for your characters to deal with the problem or challenge.

★ End your story by having the characters resolve the problem. Finish with a conclusion, which may include a statement of your theme.

★ Remember that the writing prompt may provide you with one of the basic story parts — its setting, characters, or plot — and ask you to write a story around it.

 Use a *hamburger outline, topic map,* or some other graphic organizer to get started. Brainstorm and write down as many ideas as you can think of. When you finish brainstorming, cross out any ideas you do not like.

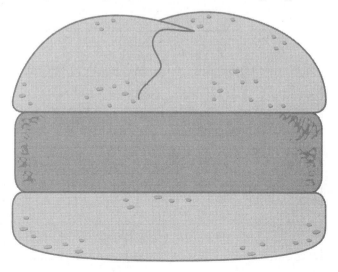

THE SETTING — WHERE AND WHEN YOUR STORY TAKES PLACE

Suppose you had to create a make-believe story about someone who faced a hardship of some kind. Let's create this story step by step to see how it's done. Begin by describing the setting.

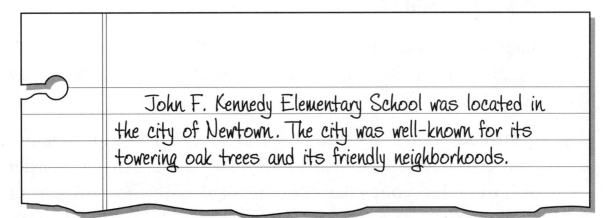

John F. Kennedy Elementary School was located in the city of Newtown. The city was well-known for its towering oak trees and its friendly neighborhoods.

WRITING YOUR OWN MAKE-BELIEVE STORY

Now write a couple of sentences giving the setting to a story of your own:

CREATING CHARACTERS IN YOUR STORY

Next, you should introduce the characters of your make-believe story. Since these characters come from your own imagination, you are the only one who knows what they look like. Give each of your main characters a name. Then describe each one as they appear in the story. To make the story more interesting, you may want to have the characters speak to each other in a conversation.

> Carson was a tall and handsome-looking third-grader. Like most of the kids in Newtown, he attended Kennedy Elementary School. Carson stood out from the rest of the students. Despite being tall, he always stayed away from fights with other students.

WRITING YOUR OWN MAKE-BELIEVE STORY

Now it's your turn. Introduce and describe one or more characters who will be a part of your story:

_____

_____

_____

_____

_____

_____

CREATING A PLOT FOR YOUR STORY

For the plot, you need to introduce some type of problem. The problem sets the stage for the action of the story. Make the problem challenging, but realistic. It could deal with natural obstacles, human relationships, or personal goals. For example,

> Some of the kids in his class thought Carson was a coward. They often picked on him because of this. Some boys began calling him a "chicken" and even made chicken noises when he walked by them.
>
> Since Carson lived near the school, he walked home each day from school with his friend Jason. One day, on their way home, Carson and Jason heard a loud rumbling noise. It was so unexpected that both boys jumped. "It sounds like an explosion," said Jason. He screamed at Carson to be sure he was heard; "We better get out of here fast."

WRITING YOUR OWN MAKE-BELIEVE STORY

*Now you should write about a **problem** or **challenge** that will set the stage for the action in your story:*

_____

_____

_____

_____

The rest of the plot should describe events as they unfold. These events should relate in some way to the central problem. Include some interesting and specific details when describing these events.

The characters and their goals may change. This will create interest among readers. Try to make readers curious to see what happens in the story.

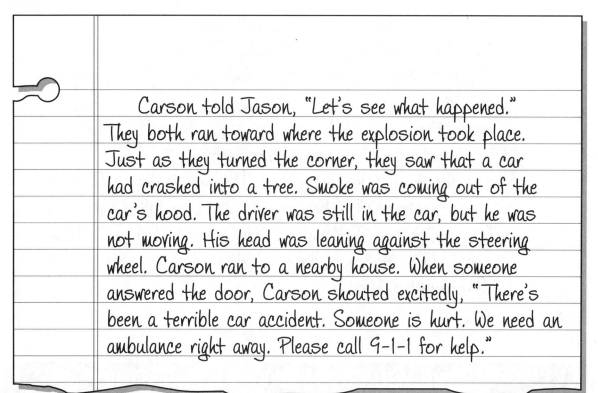

Carson told Jason, "Let's see what happened." They both ran toward where the explosion took place. Just as they turned the corner, they saw that a car had crashed into a tree. Smoke was coming out of the car's hood. The driver was still in the car, but he was not moving. His head was leaning against the steering wheel. Carson ran to a nearby house. When someone answered the door, Carson shouted excitedly, "There's been a terrible car accident. Someone is hurt. We need an ambulance right away. Please call 9-1-1 for help."

WRITING YOUR OWN MAKE-BELIEVE STORY

*Now you should give the rest of the **plot** of your story:*

_____

_____

_____

_____

CREATING A CONCLUSION TO YOUR STORY

The conclusion is the ending of your story. Your conclusion might also show how your story illustrates a general lesson in life. For example,

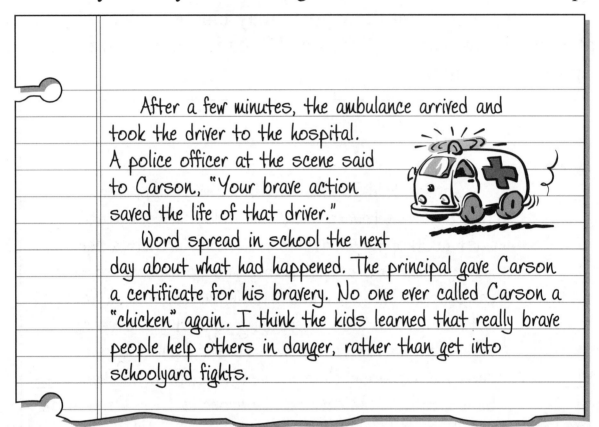

> After a few minutes, the ambulance arrived and took the driver to the hospital.
> A police officer at the scene said to Carson, "Your brave action saved the life of that driver."
> Word spread in school the next day about what had happened. The principal gave Carson a certificate for his bravery. No one ever called Carson a "chicken" again. I think the kids learned that really brave people help others in danger, rather than get into schoolyard fights.

WRITING YOUR OWN MAKE-BELIEVE STORY

*Now you should write the **conclusion** to your story:*

_____

_____

_____

_____

_____

_____

CHAPTER 20

WRITING LETTERS AND JOURNALS

Sometimes you may be required to **write a letter.** Another type of writing you may be asked to do in class is to keep a **journal.** This chapter looks at both of these — writing letters and journals.

WRITING A FRIENDLY LETTER

Although we write letters for a many reasons, they all follow a common form, with a greeting, body, and closing. A friendly letter is used for writing to a friend, relative, or pen-pal. More formal letters, such as a business letter, use a slightly different format.

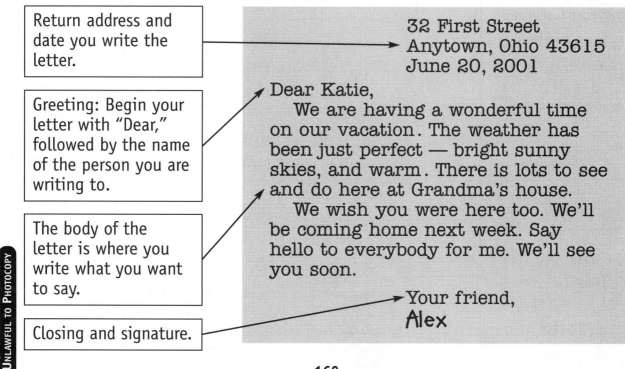

Return address and date you write the letter.

Greeting: Begin your letter with "Dear," followed by the name of the person you are writing to.

The body of the letter is where you write what you want to say.

Closing and signature.

> 32 First Street
> Anytown, Ohio 43615
> June 20, 2001
>
> Dear Katie,
>   We are having a wonderful time on our vacation. The weather has been just perfect — bright sunny skies, and warm. There is lots to see and do here at Grandma's house.
>   We wish you were here too. We'll be coming home next week. Say hello to everybody for me. We'll see you soon.
>
>   Your friend,
>   Alex

PRACTICE WRITING A FRIENDLY LETTER

Now you try it. Suppose you had a pen-pal who lived somewhere in Africa. Write your pen-pal a letter about an event that took place recently in your school or community.

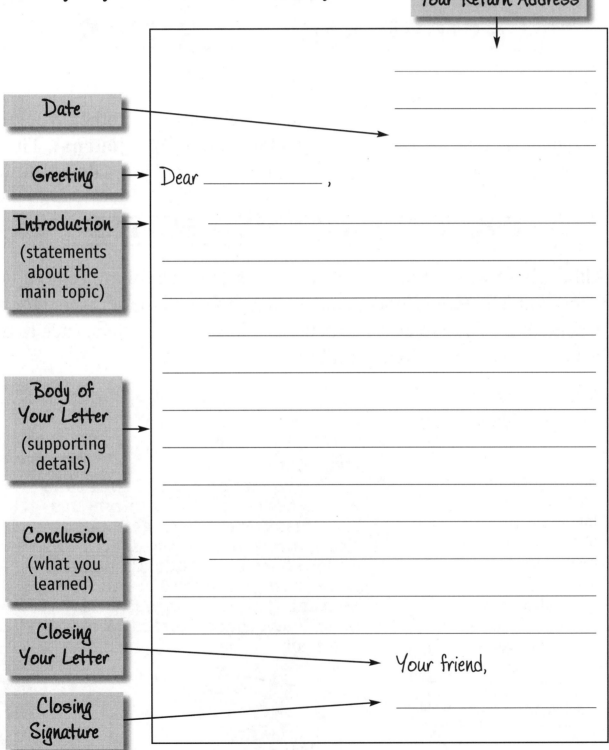

Your Return Address

Date

Greeting

Dear _____ ,

Introduction
(statements
about the
main topic)

Body of
Your Letter
(supporting
details)

Conclusion
(what you
learned)

Closing
Your Letter

Your friend,

Closing
Signature

KEEPING A JOURNAL

A **journal** is a record of your one's experiences. Journals help to keep track of events. People keep journals for a variety of reasons. The most popular journal is the *diary* — a day-to-day recording of the day's events. Professional reporters keep journals, too — to recall facts to use in their articles. A journal can even serve as a source for ideas.

HELPFUL HINTS FOR KEEPING A JOURNAL

You might keep a journal for only a few days or for many years. How often you write entries in your journal may vary. You might make an entry several times a day, on a daily basis, or only occasionally. In general, every journal entry is recorded along with the date on which it is written. For example, the following imaginary entries might have been written by an astronaut on an early space mission.

DATE	Journal Entry
January 17, 1968	The spacecraft is quite small, but comfortable. Our food looks and tastes like tooth paste. We are excited about our mission into space.
January 18, 1968	The Earth is a beautiful sight from way out here in space. We never get tired of watching from our spacecraft as the Earth turns slowly. Its green continents and blue oceans are covered by clouds. To witness a lightning storm on Earth from outer space is spectacular.
January 21, 1968	Weightlessness is a very strange experience. We pass things back and forth and watch them float around the spacecraft cabin. It's so much fun that sometimes we forget we are on an important scientific mission.

PRACTICE WRITING JOURNAL ENTRIES

Let's practice what you have just learned about making journal entries. Pretend you are on a trip visiting another country or another part of the United States. Make imaginary journal entries for three days, recording your impressions of the places you are visiting.

DATE	Journal Entry

Practice Exercises

Write a friendly letter to an imaginary pen-pal, Darrell. In your letter tell him about what you did this week at home and in school. Write your letter using this space below:

_____

_____

_____

Dear Darrell,

_____

_____

_____

_____

_____

_____

_____

_____

_____

Your friend,

_____

CHAPTER 21

A PRACTICE READING TEST

The following reading test has three reading passages divided into three sessions. Each passage will be followed by several multiple-choice questions. Some of the readings will also have a short-response and an extended-response question about what you read. You may look back at each passage as often as you like during the session. Try to time yourself. You will have **45 minutes** to complete each session. Timing yourself will help you get an idea of how long it will take to answer such questions when you take a real test. Good luck. You can begin now.

START OF SESSION 1

CARRIE ROSE HATED RED
by Susan Uhlig

Carrie Rose hated to wear red. She also disliked hot pink, neon green, and electric blue. Carrie Rose thought they made people notice her. And Carrie Rose didn't like being noticed. In fact, she worked at not being noticed. Carrie Rose sat quietly. She colored quietly. She wore quiet shoes. She never raised her hand. Even at recess Carrie was quiet so that no one would notice her.

But Carrie Rose noticed the others. Ivy always giggled. Juan raised his hand during reading. Emily chased Juan at recess. Carrie Rose wondered if they minded being noticed.

On Friday the teacher took a windup dog out of his desk. He wound it up. The little dog wagged its tail. Carrie Rose almost laughed out loud. "This is Crackers," Mr. Warner said. "He wants to go home with a student each weekend."

Oh! Come to my house, Carrie Rose thought. *You're so cute. I'll show Dad how you wag your tail!*

"Who wants to take Crackers home?" the teacher asked.

Kids near Carrie Rose raised their hands. She had never raised her hand in class. She lifted her hand from her lap to the desktop. Could she raise it higher? Too late. Mr. Warner had chosen somebody else.

CONTINUED ➔

To all the groans, Mr. Warner said, "Don't worry. Everyone will get a turn. I'll choose someone else next Friday."

All weekend Carrie Rose worried about raising her hand. Maybe she needed practice. Maybe she could get used to it. And then on Friday she could raise her hand like the others. On Monday her hand inched up for calendar person. Alex was chosen.

That night in her room, Carrie Rose practiced raising her hand in front of a mirror. It felt silly, but she thought it might help. On Tuesday her hand went halfway up. Mr. Warner called on Carrie Rose to pass out papers. With fingers trembling, Carrie Rose handed out the sheets. Some kids thanked her, others just took the paper. Carrie Rose smiled when she went back to her seat. Passing out papers was fun.

On Wednesday Carrie Rose didn't raise her hand in time to lead the Pledge of Allegiance. On Thursday her hand popped up for line leader. Ivy was chosen. Carrie Rose sighed. On Friday Carrie Rose couldn't sit still. Could she get her hand up in time? Would the teacher choose her?

Finally, Mr. Warner said, "Who wants to take Crackers home?" Carrie Rose's hand leaped straight up. So did everyone else's. She waited. And waited. What was taking so long?

CONTINUED ➡

"Carrie Rose," Mr. Warner said at last. Smiling, Carrie Rose walked to the front of the room and gently took Crackers.

"You're coming home with me!" she whispered. Carrie Rose still hates to wear red, and she still wears quiet shoes. But now Carrie Rose loves to volunteer for all kinds of things.

1. **Which sentence best summarizes the story?**
   A Carrie Rose hates to wear the color red.
   B Carrie Rose does not like to raise her hand.
   C Carrie Rose overcomes shyness by learning to raise her hand.
   D Carrie Rose is chosen to take home a mechanical dog.

2. **How was Carrie Rose different from some of her classmates?**
   A She did not like to be noticed.
   B She giggled in class.
   C She raised her hand during reading.
   D She did not like dogs.

3. **Why hadn't Carrie Rose ever raised her hand in class before?**
   A She did not speak English well.
   B She did not like to be noticed.
   C She did not want to take "Crackers" home for the weekend.
   D She did not know the answers to the teacher's questions.

4. **Which event happened first?**
   A Ivy was chosen as line leader.
   B Carrie Rose practiced raising her hand at home.
   C Carrie Rose was picked to take Crackers home.
   D Carrie Rose passed out papers in class.

5. **Who was "Crackers"?**
   A   a toy dinosaur that belonged to Juan
   B   a pet frog that belonged to Mr. Warner
   C   a new student in the class
   D   a wind-up dog that wagged its tail

6. **When Mr. Warner chose someone to take home Crackers, there were *groans*. What are *groans*?**
   A   moans and cries
   B   shouting and whistling
   C   smiles and applause
   D   hand clapping and cheers

7. **How did Carrie Rose get used to raising her hand?**
   A   She practiced at home in front of a mirror.
   B   She got her friends to help her.
   C   She practiced in front of her parents.
   D   Mr. Warner helped her after school.

8. **Why did Mr. Warner let students take Crackers home for the weekend?**
   A   It was a reward for students.
   B   It would add humor to his class lessons.
   C   It would help Carrie Rose overcome her shyness.
   D   It would allow students to learn about raising animals.

9. **Why did Carrie Rose's fingers tremble when she passed out papers in class?**
   A   She was not used to doing things that others would notice.
   B   Her teacher gave her an angry look.
   C   Other kids were making fun of her.
   D   The papers were slipping out of her hand as she walked.

10. **Why wasn't Carrie Rose chosen by Mr. Warner to lead the Pledge of Allegiance?**

   A He did it in alphabetical order, and it wasn't her turn.

   B She did not volunteer to do it.

   C She did not raise her hand in time.

   D She did not know how to lead the Pledge of Allegiance.

11. **What is the theme of this story?**

   A A person can overcome problems like shyness.

   B Shy people are just like everybody else.

   C Teachers can help you overcome all of your problems.

   D Volunteering is important in life.

EXTENDED-RESPONSE QUESTION

Show how Carrie Rose changes in the course of this story. Explain your answer using details from the story.

_____

_____

_____

_____

_____

_____

_____

STOP

START OF SESSION 2

HAPPY BIRTHDAY, BASKETBALL!
by Charles Davis

It was the summer of 1891. Born in Canada, James Naismith had just become an instructor at the YMCA Training School in Springfield, Massachusetts. He had been given a challenge by his boss: to invent a new game. It had to be easy to learn and easy to play indoors during the winter. The game couldn't be rough or dangerous. Most important, it had to be fun and played to the highest standards of good sportsmanship.

James Naismith and his wife stand next to the peach baskets originally used as the game's goals.

At first, James tried taking out-door games the students knew and bringing them indoors. But indoor rugby and soccer were too rough to play in a small gym. People could get hurt. When his students played lacrosse in the gym, they broke the windows. With only a day left before he had to report the new game to his boss, James still hadn't come up with the right game.

So he started thinking. Why not take parts from different games and make a new one? From soccer he chose the large ball. From lacrosse, he took the idea of a goal.

He decided to put the goal up high so it could not be easily defended. From football came the idea of passing the ball to move it down the court.

CONTINUED →

As he slept that night, he dreamed of the new game. The next morning, he wrote down thirteen rules. Then he went to look for something to use as goals.

He asked building repairman Pop Stebbins for two boxes, but Pop couldn't find any. "I have two peach baskets in the storeroom; will they do?" Pop said. James took the baskets and tacked them to the jogging track along the gym's ten-foot-high balcony.

As the students entered the gym, James explained the rules to them. He divided the eighteen students into two teams. Then the world's first basketball game got under way. The students had a blast! It was a little confusing at first. Nobody really knew the rules yet. When the game was over, the score was 1–0. All the students could talk about was how much fun the new game was. They decided it needed a name.

The players who played the first game of basketball at the YMCA Training School. Naismith is in a business suit.

"How about Naismith ball," young Frank Mahan suggested. "You invented it, it should have your name." James laughed, saying nobody would play a game called "Naismith ball." Frank responded, "How about basketball?" James agreed.

In the years following that game, basketball has changed in many ways. Bouncing the ball, or "dribbling," was added as another way to move the ball down the court. Peach baskets were replaced with metal baskets, but they still didn't have open bottoms until 1912.

CONTINUED ▶

Soon the game became the most popular activity at the YMCA. Today, it's one of the world's favorite games. James Naismith would be pleased to see modern players soar through the air for a jam or thread a pass through the lane. But he'd be even happier to see them shaking hands as friends when the game ended.

1. **What is the article mostly about?**
   A the life of James Naismith
   B how the game of basketball was invented
   C the importance of basketball in society
   D how the game of basketball has changed

2. **The story tells us: "The students had a *blast*." What does *blast* mean in this sentence?**
   A a loud explosion   C an exciting time
   B danger   D a noisy outburst

3. **Which event in the history of basketball took place last?**
   A Peach baskets were replaced with metal ones.
   B The baskets were given open bottoms.
   C Dribbling was added.
   D The game was named basketball.

4. **Basketball is a favorite American sport, but its inventor was born in**
   A Canada
   B Massachusetts
   C Ireland
   D Mexico

5. What was the job of Pop Stebbins?
   A athletic director
   B coach
   C repairman
   D teacher

6. When was the game of basketball invented?
   A 1891
   B 1900
   C 1912
   D 1925

7. Which is a factual statement about the game of basketball?
   A Basketball has been played for over 100 years.
   B Basketball was originally called Naismith ball.
   C When it was first invented, the game of basketball had no rules.
   D Basketball has remained unchanged since it was first invented.

8. What led James Naismith to invent the game of basketball?
   A He came up with the game to relieve his boredom.
   B His boss challenged him to invent a new game.
   C He hated the winter and wanted to find a game to play indoors.
   D His job at the YMCA was to create new sports games.

9. In what way is basketball similar today to when it was invented?
   A Fun and sportsmanship are still important parts of the game.
   B The game remains rough and dangerous.
   C Players move the ball by dribbling.
   D The basket consists of a metal hoop and net.

10. **Why did Naismith tack the peach baskets to the ten-foot high rail of the gym's balcony jogging track?**

   A He wanted both teams to jump when scoring.

   B It was the only place to hang the peach baskets.

   C He put the goals up high to make it difficult to defend.

   D It would be impossible for a player to damage the baskets.

SHORT-RESPONSE QUESTION

What are two ways the game of basketball has changed since the first game was played? Use information from the passage in your answer.

_____

_____

_____

_____

_____

_____

_____

_____

_____

STOP

START OF SESSION 3

TASHIRA'S TURN
edited by William J. Bennett

One day during recess Tashira found her mother in the school-yard with a bucket of soap and water. She was scrubbing a wall where someone had written some ugly words and pictures. "Mama!" Tashira called. "What are you doing?"

"I'm helping your teachers keep the school clean," her mother said. When Tashira asked if it was hard work, her mother said, "It's nothing. It's just my turn to help, you see."

The school bell rang. Tashira's mom went back to scrubbing the wall. All the ugly words and pictures ran to the ground, where they turned into puddles of silver and gold.

The next day Tashira was walking past her church, when she heard voices in the sky. She looked up and saw her teacher on the roof! "Hello, Mrs. Jenkins," Tashira called. "What're you doing up there?"

"We're helping Reverend Wilburn," her teacher proclaimed. "The steeple needs a fresh coat of paint."

"That's brave of you to climb so high," Tashira shouted.

"Its not so high," her teacher said. "Besides, it's our turn to help."

CONTINUED →

The next morning, Tashira was skipping rope when she saw Reverend Wilburn with a basket under his arm.

"Hi, Reverend Wilburn," she called. "Where are you going with that big basket?"

"I'm taking dinner to Officer Hamlette and his family." Reverend Wilburn smiled. "Mrs. Hamlette just had a baby. Everyone in the neighborhood is taking turns bringing her a meal." He lifted the basket's cover so Tashira could peek inside.

"It's so kind of you to cook such a nice, juicy turkey," she said.

"Oh, it's just my turn to help, that's all," said Reverend Wilburn.

The next day Tashira went to the park. The swings were still because a gang of boys were scaring the little children away. Then Officer Hamlette came along. When the bad boys saw him, they ran away. Officer Hamlette stood on the corner watching them go. Before long, all the little children came out to play.

"Thanks, Officer Hamlette," called Tashira. "The little children were scared to play until you came along."

"Oh, its nothing," smiled Officer Hamlette. "It's just my turn to help, that's all."

The next morning, Tashira was riding her bike when she heard a voice crying. She looked and saw smoke pouring out of an open window. "Someone needs help," she thought. She jumped off her bike and ran to the window. Smoke stung her eyes, and she wanted to turn away, but she glimpsed a little boy inside crying for his mother.

CONTINUED →

"I'll take you to her," Tashira told him. She reached through the window and pulled him out.

"Keisha's still in the house," he cried. Tashira looked through the window but the smoke was so thick, she could not see anything inside.

"Wait here," she cried. "We need more help." Tashira ran down the street. A moment later she was back with Officer Hamlette. He disappeared into the smoke. Tashira waited and waited. He was gone an awfully long time. When he finally came out of the house, he had a little girl in his arms. Now fire engines were roaring down the street with their sirens screaming. The firemen dashed into the house carrying long hoses.

The children's mother came running. "Oh my babies," she cried.

Reverend Wilburn came running. "Tashira, you're a hero!" he shouted. Then Tashira's teacher came running, "She's a hero!" she shouted. "Tashira's a hero."

A big crowd gathered around. Tashira's own mother was there to give her a big hug, too. "You're a hero, Tashira!" they all shouted.

Tashira just shook her head and smiled. "I'm not a hero," she said. "It's just my turn to help, that's all." But everyone said she was a hero, all the same.

1. **What is the story mostly about?**
   A A girl sees everyone helping others and does the same when it's her turn.
   B A police officer helps children in the playground.
   C A teacher helps paint the church steeple.
   D A girl saves a young boy from a burning house.

2. **Which event in the story happens first?**
   A Tashira saves Keisha's brother.
   B Officer Hamlette gets a gang of boys to leave the playground.
   C Mrs. Jenkins helps Reverend Wilburn paint the steeple.
   D Tashira's mother scrubs a schoolyard wall.

3. **Why does Mrs. Jenkins decide to help Reverend Wilburn?**
   A She owes him a favor.
   B It is her turn to help out.
   C Reverend Wilburn is afraid to climb so high.
   D She needs to earn extra money on the weekends.

4. **Which sentence best describes the people of Tashira's community?**
   A They are very wealthy.
   B They try to avoid hard work.
   C They have a policeman because of frequent crimes.
   D They assist other people who need help.

5. **Why does Reverend Wilburn take dinner to Officer Hamlette and his family?**
   A The church provides food for those too poor to buy their own.
   B Officer Hamlette and his family have not eaten for days.
   C Mrs. Hamlette just had a baby.
   D Mrs. Hamlette was badly hurt in a fire.

6. **Why did Tashira reach through the window of the smoking house?**

   A She heard a girl in the house call for help.

   B She saw a little boy in the house crying.

   C She was visiting the people in the house.

   D She wanted to show everyone she was a real hero.

SHORT-RESPONSE QUESTION

How does Tashira help to save Keisha? Use information from the reading passage in your answer.

_____

_____

_____

_____

7. **"We're helping Reverend Wilburn," her teacher *proclaimed*. In this sentence, what does *proclaimed* mean?**

   A announce publicly

   B refuse to help

   C favor one side

   D show ownership

8. **Why did people in the story call Tashira a hero?**

   A She helped save two children's lives.

   B She ran into a burning house.

   C She pushed past Officer Hamlette to save the baby.

   D She helped save most of the main characters in the story.

9. **Why did Tashira tell everyone she was NOT a hero?**

   A In her neighborhood, people helped others when it was their turn.

   B She had run away to get help instead of rushing into the house.

   C She did not really know what to do during the fire.

   D She had been afraid to save Keisha.

10. **What is the main theme of this story?**

   A Never leave children alone if they are playing with matches.

   B We should help out others.

   C Always be careful around a fire.

   D Never judge people by the way they dress.

EXTENDED-RESPONSE QUESTION

Why did people think Tashira was a hero? Explain your answer using details from the story.

_____

_____

_____

_____

_____

_____

_____

_____

STOP

CHAPTER 22

A PRACTICE WRITING TEST

The following writing test consists of two 45-minute sessions. Your teacher may decide to have both sessions on the same day, or your teacher may have each session on a separate day. Each session has two writing prompts. Choose **one** writing prompt during each session. Then write an essay or story in response to that prompt. Don't answer both prompts. Only your answer to one of the prompts will be scored. If needed, extra paper will be provided by your teacher. Your final draft will be scored on the following:

☐ focus ☐ support ☐ organization
☐ use of writing conventions

Now turn to Session 1. Good luck!

START OF SESSION 1

CHOOSE ONE OF THE FOLLOWING TOPICS TO WRITE ABOUT:

★ Have you ever been in a situation in which you didn't quite feel comfortable or felt like a stranger? Describe that situation and tell what you did.

★ Tell about your most interesting friend. Tell who it is and explain why you find this friend to be so interesting.

Use the space below to outline your composition. Then write the first draft of your composition on the next page. Once you finish revising your draft, you should write your final composition.

Pre-Writing

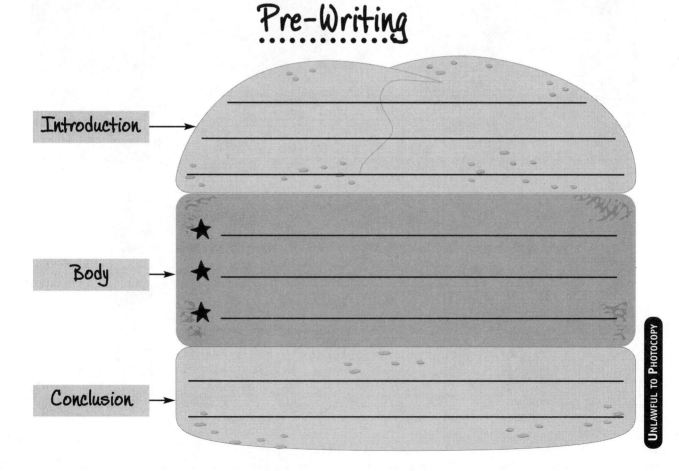

Introduction

Body

★

★

★

Conclusion

Rough Draft

Use the space below to write your first draft.

Final, Edited Version

Use the space below to write your final, edited version.

STOP

START OF SESSION 2

CHOOSE ONE OF THE FOLLOWING TOPICS TO WRITE ABOUT:

★ Imagine that you could make up your own holiday. Tell what holiday you would make up and explain why.

★ All of us have something we enjoy doing most of all. Tell about your favorite activity, and explain why this activity gives you such enjoyment.

Use the space below to outline your composition. Then, write the first draft of your composition on the next page. Once you finish revising your draft, you should write your final composition.

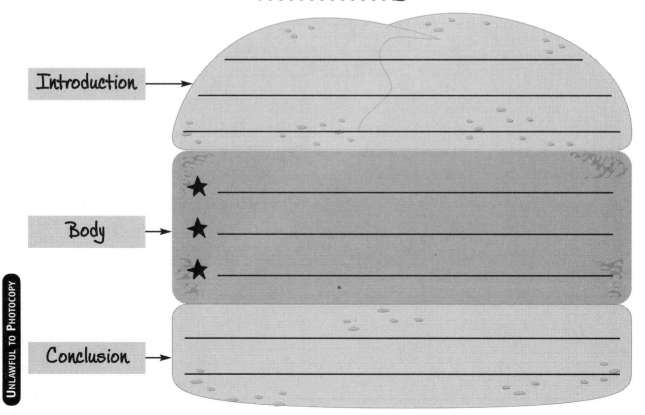

Pre-Writing

Introduction

Body

★
★
★

Conclusion

Rough Draft

Use the space below to write your first draft.

Final, Edited Version

Use the space below to write your final, edited version.

STOP

INTERPRETING DATA

A classroom, school, or state-wide test may have a reading passage with information, known as **data,** presented in graphic or visual form. This *Appendix* will examine each of the major forms of data that might appear in a reading passage.

MAPS

A **map** is a drawing that represents a geographical area. There is almost no limit to the kind of information that can be shown on a map.

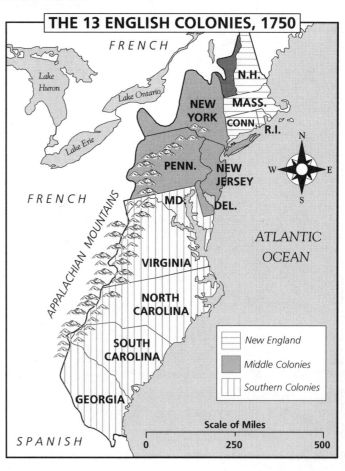

THE 13 ENGLISH COLONIES, 1750

FRENCH

Lake Huron

Lake Ontario

Lake Erie

N.H.

MASS.

NEW YORK

CONN.

R.I.

FRENCH

APPALACHIAN MOUNTAINS

PENN.

NEW JERSEY

MD.

DEL.

VIRGINIA

NORTH CAROLINA

SOUTH CAROLINA

GEORGIA

ATLANTIC OCEAN

N W E S

New England

Middle Colonies

Southern Colonies

Scale of Miles

0   250   500

SPANISH

KEYS TO UNDERSTANDING A MAP

★ **Read the Title.** The title of the map tells you what kind of information is presented. For example, the title of the map above is: *The 13 English Colonies, 1750.* This map shows the location of the English colonies in North America in the year 1750.

★ **Look at the Legend.** The legend unlocks the information on the map. It identifies what each symbol represents. For example, in this map:

- **horizontal lines** ▤ show the location of the colonies of New England.

- **light gray areas** ▢ show the location of the Middle Colonies.

- **vertical lines** ▥ show the location of the Southern Colonies.

CHECKING YOUR UNDERSTANDING

Name **two** English colonies located in New England:

1. _____

2. _____

Name **one** of the Southern Colonies: _____

GRAPHS

Graphs generally use bars or lines to represent amounts.

A **bar graph** is a chart made up of parallel bars with different lengths. A bar graph is often used to make a comparison of two or more things.

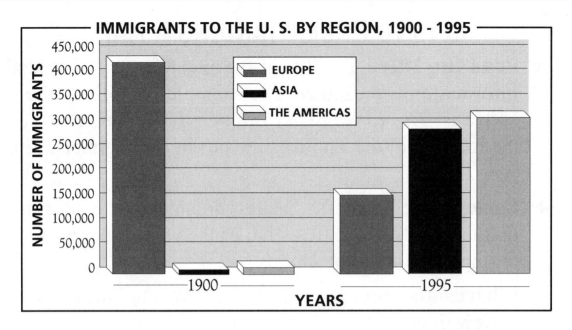

KEYS TO UNDERSTANDING A BAR GRAPH

★ **Read the Title.** The title tells you the topic of the graph.

★ **Look at the Legend.** The legend shows what each bar represents. For example, the

- **gray bars** represent *Europe*

- **black bars** represent *Asia*

- **light gray bars** represent the *Americas* (*North, Central, and South America*)

★ **Examine the Bars.** The length of each bar represents a specific amount. The number on the line at the left of the graph gives the number that a particular bar represents.

CHECKING YOUR UNDERSTANDING

According to the bar graph above, about how many immigrants came to the United States from Asia in 1995?

_____

PIE CHARTS

A **pie chart,** also called a **circle graph,** is a circle divided into sections of different sizes. Each slice is a fraction of the whole pie. If you add up all the slices they will equal 100%. Pie charts are often used to show the relationship between a whole and its parts.

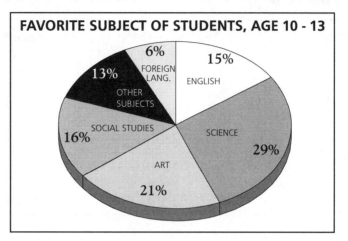

FAVORITE SUBJECT OF STUDENTS, AGE 10 - 13

KEYS TO UNDERSTANDING A PIE CHART

★ **Read the Title.** The title tells you the overall topic.

★ **Examine the Legend.** Sometimes a pie chart has a legend showing what each slice of the pie represents. If the information is shown on the slices, as on this pie chart, a legend is not needed.

★ **Look at the Slices of the Pie.** In this pie, each slice represents the favorite subject of some students. For example, 29% of students, ages 10 to 13, chose science as their favorite subject.

CHECKING YOUR UNDERSTANDING

Which subject was least popular among students, ages 10 to 13?

_____

TABLES

A **table** is an arrangement of words or numbers in columns. A table is often used to organize large amounts of information so that facts can be easily located and compared.

CHARITY GIVING IN THE UNITED STATES, 1991–1995

Year	Individuals	Businesses
1991	$96.10 billion	$5.62 billion
1992	$98.38 billion	$5.92 billion
1993	$102.13 billion	$6.26 billion
1994	$104.53 billion	$6.88 billion
1995	$116.23 billion	$7.40 billion

KEYS TO UNDERSTANDING A TABLE

★ **Read the Title.** The title of the table tells you its overall topic.

★ **Look at the Categories.** Each table is made up of various categories of information. These categories are named in the column headings across the top of the table.

★ **Finding Information.** To find specific information, you must find where the columns and rows of information intersect or cross.

CHECKING YOUR UNDERSTANDING

Identify the categories used in this table: _____

Name the year that individuals contributed the most money to charity and the amount they gave.

Year: _____   Amount: _____